U.S.-Soviet Cultural
Exchanges, 1958–1986

About the Book and Author

The U.S.-USSR Cultural Agreement signed at the Geneva summit in 1985 signaled the resumption of a broad range of cultural exchanges suspended in 1980 after the Soviet invasion of Afghanistan. Mr. Richmond describes the history of the various areas of exchange—in the performing arts, popular media, academia, public diplomacy, science and technology, sports, and tourism—analyzing how they have evolved over the past twenty-eight years and how they are conducted in the two countries. He explains, for example, how the U.S. government and the private sector joined forces in 1958 to conduct exchanges with the Soviet Union under an intergovernmental cultural agreement—the first ever for the United States—and how, over the years, the impetus for exchanges has shifted from the government to the private sector and to individual U.S. citizens. In addition, Mr. Richmond provides an account of U.S. government procedures for assessing Soviet proposals for exchanges in science and technology and outlines the difficulties that exchanges with the Soviets entail, including visa problems, defections, travel restrictions, and technology transfer.

Yale Richmond, a veteran of thirty years in the U.S. Foreign Service, worked for more than twenty years on exchanges with the Soviet Union and Eastern Europe. He is currently on the staff of the National Endowment for Democracy.

U.S.-Soviet Cultural Exchanges, 1958–1986

Who Wins?

Yale Richmond

Foreword by Marshall D. Shulman

Westview Press / Boulder and London

Westview Special Studies on the Soviet Union and Eastern Europe

---

This Westview softcover edition is printed on acid-free paper and bound in softcovers that carry the highest rating of the National Association of State Textbook Administrators, in consultation with the Association of American Publishers and the Book Manufacturers' Institute.

Copyright © 1987 by Westview Press, Inc.

Published in 1987 in the United States of America by Westview Press, Inc.; Frederick A. Praeger, Publisher; 5500 Central Avenue, Boulder, Colorado 80301

Library of Congress Cataloging-in-Publication Data
Richmond, Yale.
    U.S.-Soviet cultural exchanges, 1958–1986.
    (Westview special studies on the Soviet Union and
Eastern Europe)
    Bibliography: p.
    Includes index.
    1. United States—Relations—Soviet Union. 2. Soviet
Union—Relations—United States. I. Title. II. Title:
U.S.-Soviet cultural exchanges, 1958–1986. III. Series.
E183.8.S65R55 1987   303.4'8273'047   86-18985
ISBN 0-8133-7275-5

This book was produced without formal editing by the publisher.

Printed and bound in the United States of America

The paper used in this publication meets the requirements of the American National Standard for Permanence of Paper for Printed Library Materials Z39.48-1984.

6 5 4 3 2 1

Contents

Foreword

Cultural exchanges between the United States and the Soviet Union are full of dilemmas and trade-offs for both sides.

The basic problem has involved learning how to mesh the centralized and controlled institutions on the Soviet side with the pluralistic institutions of the United States. The learning process has been tortuous, but it has been propelled by the quite different self-interests of the two sides and aided by persistence and ingenuity, and a fairly workable system has emerged.

At the governmental level, the propelling interest on the Soviet side has been to accelerate the laggard sector of science and technology in the Soviet economy. On the American side, the governmental purpose has been to induce changes in the Soviet system. At the level of the individuals involved, the driving motivation has been curiosity; purposeful learning about each other's societies, institutions and politics; and a faith that the substitution of knowledge for primitive stereotypes would somehow, over the long run, take some of the danger out of the U.S.-Soviet relationship.

For all those who may be involved in these exchanges—scholars, students, tourists, discussion groups, artistic groups, museum exhibitors—and for all those who wish to think further about the place of the cultural exchanges in the U.S.-Soviet relationship, Yale Richmond has performed an invaluable service in this book. It will be an indispensable reference, a historical record, and a starting point for those who wish to study the role and management of cultural exchanges in more depth.

Well-qualified by his two decades of experience in the government negotiating and managing exchange agreements, Mr. Richmond has assembled the long and sometimes painful record of how these two societies and systems groped for ways to send their people across the barricades of their different institutions and conflicting purposes. He has performed this task judiciously, without illusions about the difficulties, but with the underlying conviction that, properly managed, exchanges can have positive benefits for the people of both countries.

It is of course impossible to measure the benefits of bilateral exchanges, particularly on the Soviet side. Those of us who have been involved in U.S.-Soviet exchanges since they were first formalized almost thirty years ago have formed strong impressions of the useful residual effects of these experiences on both sides. The changes we have witnessed in Soviet society over the past three decades have, without a doubt, been stimulated by multitudinous contacts, however gingerly they have been circumscribed. In my own field—the scholarly study of the Soviet Union—there is ample evidence of the quantum leap gained as a result of the opportunity for our scholars and students to spend prolonged periods of time in the Soviet Union. Our research is no longer dependent on the often cramped printed materials available to us. Direct contact has given us insights into the way the Soviet system works and has enabled us to plug into the oral levels of discourse in that country, which are so much more complex and rich than what can be printed in Soviet journals and books.

Stimulated and informed by Mr. Richmond's account, readers will be better able to face the questions and problems that still remain in the management of cultural exchanges. What is the proper role of government in relation to the voluntary coordination of private institutions in the United States that will enable us to manage these exchanges fairly but without intruding on the proper prerogatives of the private sector in America's pluralistic society? In what cases are reciprocal tit-for-tat restrictions necessary, and when are they self-defeating? How can we protect access to legitimate security information in this country without impeding the flow of information that is vital to our own scientific research?

Mr. Richmond does not attempt to provide categorical answers to such questions, but his account is a useful starting point for all of us who need to grapple with these problems.

Marshall D. Shulman
Adlai E. Stevenson Professor Emeritus
of International Relations
and former director, W. Averell Harriman
Institute for Advanced Study of the Soviet Union,
Columbia University

Preface

The signature of a new U.S.-Soviet cultural agreement at the Reagan-Gorbachev Geneva Summit on November 21, 1985, called public attention to this little-known and less-understood aspect of Soviet-American relations.

This study, written for the general public as well as the foreign affairs specialist, is an attempt to explain how cultural exchanges with the Soviet Union began in the late 1950s, how they have evolved since their inception and how they are conducted today.

I hope that the information contained in these pages will have an impact on future exchanges as well as on the policies of the U.S. government and the private sector that govern them. I also hope it will foster a greater appreciation of how far we have come and how far we have yet to go before normal cultural relations with the Soviet Union become a reality.

I have drawn on my more than twenty years of work with the Soviet Union and the countries of Eastern Europe on exchanges in culture, education, information and science, including the negotiation of sixteen intergovernmental agreements in these fields as well as assignments at the American Embassies in Moscow and Warsaw and at the Department of State, the United States Information Agency and the Commission on Security and Cooperation in Europe of the U.S. Congress.

Because of my personal involvement in these exchanges, I have attempted to distance myself from the events described. However, if my firm belief in the value of exchanges shows through, so be it.

My greatest challenge in preparing this study has been how to make the incredibly complex subject of Soviet-American exchanges, about which I know perhaps too many details, intelligible to the general reader. I hope I have succeeded.

I also hope that this study will help to explain to the public what it is like to negotiate with the Soviets and to work with them on matters of mutual interest. In this respect, the trials and tribulations of cultural exchanges are but a microcosm of the world of Soviet-American relations.

The events described here are not atypical.   Rather, they are examples of what all Americans experience, both in and out of government, in the fascinating but frustrating field of Soviet-American relations.

Yale Richmond
Washington, D.C.

Acknowledgments

This study is an expanded, revised and updated edition of a monograph published in 1984 by the Kennan Institute for Advanced Russian Studies, Woodrow Wilson International Center for Scholars. I am indebted to Herbert J. Ellison, former Secretary of the Kennan Institute, and his staff, Bradford P. Johnson in particular, for their assistance in publishing that monograph.

Bruce Kellison of Westview Press was very helpful in providing advice and other assistance in seeing this work through to completion. Evan A. Raynes of the Kennan Institute came to my rescue many times on word processing problems.

To my former Foreign Service colleagues who made helpful suggestions, I am most grateful. These include Nicholas G. Andrews, Irene G. Carstones, Guy E. Coriden, Gregory Guroff, Edward Hurwitz, John K. Jacobs, Boris H. Klosson, Byron B. Morton, Joseph A. Presel, Robert L. Richards, Jaroslav J. Verner, Paul E. Wheeler and Arthur I. Wortzel.

I am also indebted to Phillips Ruopp, formerly of the Charles F. Kettering Foundation; Toby Trister Gati, United Nations Association of the United States of America; Phillip Stewart, Ohio State University; Kenneth Clark, Motion Picture Association of America, Cord Hansen-Sturm, First Family of Travel; Townsend Hoopes, Association of American Publishers; Martin P. Levin, formerly Times Mirror Co.; Glenn E. Schweitzer, National Academy of Sciences; and Gerson Sher, National Science Foundation.

On student and scholarly exchanges, I received counsel from Allen H. Kassof, Daniel Matuszewski and Dorothy Knapp, International Research and Exchanges Board; Leon Twarog, Ohio State University; Dan Davidson, American Council of Teachers of Russian; John Skillman, Council on International Educational Exchange; and William James, formerly Council on International Exchange of Scholars.

I also wish to acknowledge the writings of others on U.S.-Soviet exchanges, especially Alexander Dallin, Stanford University; Loren

Graham, Massachusetts Institute of Technology; and Linda Lubrano, American University.

To Robert F. Byrnes, Indiana University, I am indebted for his comprehensive "Soviet-American Academic Exchanges, 1958–1975," which provided much useful data on the early years of exchanges, and for his challenging and critical views on the role of government in academic exchanges.

The document NSC 5607, "East-West Exchanges," and the Department of State report, "Survey of U.S. Educational and Cultural Exchanges with the Soviet Union and Eastern Europe," were declassified and released under the Freedom of Information Act.

The manuscript of my Kennan Institute monograph was submitted to the Department of State, which found, on April 24, 1984, that there was no objection to its publication.

The views expressed are, of course, my own.

Y.R.

1

Overview

Introduction

"Who wins, we or the Russians?" I was often asked when I worked on Soviet-American exchanges at the State Department in the 1970s, the détente years when these exchanges greatly expanded. Some Americans regard cultural exchanges with the Soviets as a competition in which points are scored, tallied and one side or the other wins. And the communists, they argue, would not be promoting cultural exchanges so eagerly unless they had ulterior motives.

Defenders of exchanges point to the need to communicate, to maintain a public dialogue, and for Americans to learn more about the Soviet Union, and Soviets to learn more about the United States, not necessarily to resolve differences but to understand them better and to make more rational decisions on issues dividing the two countries.

Critics cite the built-in disadvantages to a pluralist and open society in attempting to cooperate with a totalitarian and closed society, the unequal conditions for exchanges in the two countries, the freedom of travel and access to Americans for Soviet visitors in the United States and the controls on travel and access to Soviets for Americans in the Soviet Union, the disparity in mutual benefits and, in some exchanges, reciprocity.

Debate over these issues has continued since these exchanges began in 1958, and debate will undoubtedly continue in the future as each U.S. administration considers which exchanges we should have with the Soviets and under what conditions.

This study will explain how these exchanges began, how they have developed over the past twenty-eight years, and how they are conducted in 1986, as the United States begins another chapter in its exchanges with the Soviet Union.

The Cultural Agreement

The first U.S.-USSR exchanges agreement was signed in 1958, the Lacy-Zarubin agreement, named after the two chief negotiators and signatories, William S. B. Lacy, President Eisenhower's Special Assistant on East-West Exchanges, and Georgy Z. Zarubin, Soviet Ambassador to the United States.[1]

Commonly called the cultural agreement, this two-year agreement, and those which followed it periodically, was actually a general agreement which included exchanges in science and technology, agriculture, medicine and public health, radio and television, motion pictures, exhibitions, publications, government, youth, athletics, scholarly research, culture and tourism. Included also was an understanding, in principle, to establish direct air service between the two countries. The agreement was intended to encompass all exchanges between the two countries. As an executive agreement, rather than a treaty, it did not require Senate ratification.

The full title of the agreement was "Agreement between the United States of America and the Union of Soviet Socialist Republics on Exchanges in the Cultural, Technical and Educational Fields." The relative importance of science and technology became more evident in the second agreement, signed in 1959, when the word "cooperation" was added, and science and technology were moved ahead of culture and education. The new title read "Agreement between . . . for Cooperation in Exchanges in the Scientific, Technical, Educational and Cultural Fields in 1960-61."[2]

The third agreement, signed in 1962, added the phrase, ". . . and Other Fields."[3] This remained the pattern until 1973 when the title was further amended to read "General Agreement between . . . on Contacts, Exchanges and Cooperation in Scientific, Technical, Educational, Cultural and Other Fields."[4] This was also the title of the agreement signed at the Reagan-Gorbachev summit meeting in 1985.[5]

Signing such an agreement in 1958 was a new departure for the United States. Many of the activities included in the agreement are, for the most part, the responsibility of the private sector—science and technology, radio and television, motion pictures, publishing, youth activities, education, culture and tourism—and government activity in many of these fields is only peripheral. In the Soviet Union, by contrast, all of these activities are governmental. Here at the start was one of the many difficulties which would emerge as two very different societies attempted to establish contacts and cooperation over a broad range of activities.

There was no precedent on the U.S. side for such an agreement. Thousands of foreign students come to the United States each year without intergovernmental agreements, as well as specialists in industry, science, culture, athletics and other fields covered by the agreement.

Why then was such an agreement signed? How could the federal government agree to regulate, in its relations with another government, the international activities of U.S. universities, industry, and media and our many and varied cultural institutions?

The simple answer is that the Soviets wanted an agreement, and they made it a condition to having exchanges. The Soviets like to put things on paper, signed by their political authorities at an appropriately high level. And in a country where the government and communist party control practically everything, it would be inconceivable to conduct exchanges with another country, particularly the leader of the capitalist West, without a formal agreement which spells out exactly what will be exchanged and under what conditions. Moreover, with their highly centralized government and central planning, the Soviets claim they need an agreement to enable their participating ministries and agencies to budget in advance for exchanges and to make plans for the agreed activities.

The Soviet agencies responsible for exchanges and the officials who direct them also need the protective cover of an agreement to justify their exchanges with the United States. It was only five years after Stalin's death when the first Soviet-American cultural agreement was signed, and no one in the Soviet Union could say—then or even now—whether Soviet policy might again change. Finally, the Soviets, in general, like bilateral agreements with the United States for these agreements, in their view, lend legitimacy to the Soviet regime and imply equality between the two superpowers.

There was some reluctance on the U.S. side to break precedent and sign an agreement, but there was also high interest in government and private circles in engaging the Soviets in exchanges, in an attempt to break down the barriers separating the two countries and to make a start in normalizing relations.

The United States, during World War II, had proposed a broad program of cultural and information exchanges to the Soviet Union, but without success.[6] A Rockefeller Foundation offer, in 1944, of fellowships to Soviets for study in the United States went unanswered. After the war, in October 1945, the Department of State offered to exchange performing artists, exhibitions and students, and it invited the Red Army Chorus to tour in the United States. Again, there was no Soviet response. In the 1960s and 1970s by contrast, the Soviets several times proposed to send the Red Army Chorus, but the State Department response in those years was a firm no because of the Red Army's actions in Hungary in 1956 and in Czechoslovakia in 1968.

The Soviets opened the door slightly in 1955, only two years after Stalin's death. A U.S. company of "Porgy and Bess," on tour in Europe, was invited to perform in Moscow and Leningrad, and the Boston Symphony Orchestra the following year. A few exchanges in agriculture, medicine and journalism took place over the next two years. Some members of Congress, religious leaders and American businessmen traveled to the Soviet Union, and American scholars began to visit as tourists, the only way they could go in those years. Soviet pianist Emil Gilels performed in the United States, the first Soviet artist to appear here in the postwar period, and he was followed by violinist David Oistrakh.

At the 1955 Geneva Foreign Ministers Conference, France, the United Kingdom and the United States proposed to the Soviet Union a seventeen-point program to remove barriers to normal exchanges in the information media, culture, education, books and publications, science, sports and tourism.[7] The initiative was rejected by Foreign Minister Molotov who accused the West of interference in Soviet internal affairs. Actually, the Soviets were interested in some of the proposals, and Molotov indicated that the Soviet Union might be agreeable to concluding bilateral or multilateral agreements which "could reflect what is of particular interest to the countries concerned."[8] The Soviets also made it clear that travel abroad, as proposed by the West, was "an instrument of Soviet policy."[9]

Further developments had to await the Twentieth Party Congress in February 1956 where Khrushchev attacked Stalin and signaled a change in Soviet policies which included peaceful coexistence and increased contacts with the West.

After the Congress, the Soviets moved swiftly to establish exchanges with the West. Cultural agreements were signed with Belgium and Norway later in 1956, and with France in 1957. Negotiations with the United States began on October 29, 1957, and an exchange agreement was signed on January 28, 1958.

Soviet Objectives

The Soviets don't talk publicly about their objectives, and there is no Soviet equivalent to our Freedom of Information Act. One can only speculate, therefore, what prompted them to make a radical departure from past practice, to permit their scientists, scholars and cultural personalities to travel and study in the United States, and to open their borders to similar visitors from the West. But after twenty-eight years of exchanges with the Soviet Union and the opportunities they have provided to observe Soviet interests and priorities, their objectives are not so difficult to make out.

Access to U.S. science and technology has been and remains the main Soviet objective. It is easier and quicker to acquire technology through exchanges, or to purchase it through commercial arrangements, than to develop it at home. Russia historically has had a long tradition of acquiring technology and administrative know-how from the West, dating back to Ivan III and Peter the Great. So the first cultural agreement with the United States, and all subsequent agreements until 1972, included up front a section on exchanges of delegations in technology for visits to industrial facilities in the two countries. Most of these science and technology exchanges were spun off, in 1972, 1973 and 1974, to the eleven cooperative agreements which were signed at the three Nixon-Brezhnev summit meetings.

Soviet priorities were also evident in the remarks of Ambassador Zarubin at the opening of the exchange negotiations in 1957. The Soviets, he said, "have in mind an exchange of delegations in the following industries: metallurgical, mining, automobile, chemical, radio, tool engineering, plastic, electric power and others, as well as specialists in the construction of different industrial enterprises, planning and construction of towns, and construction of bridges." Also mentioned by Zarubin were exchanges in agriculture, including cattle breeding, vegetable growing and other fields.[10]

Political objectives were also high among Soviet priorities. Peaceful coexistence was the favored Soviet slogan in the late 1950s, and cooperation was sought with the advanced capitalist countries. Zarubin, in his remarks, also hoped that exchanges would "contribute to the normalization and improvement of relations and the relaxation of international tension" and "the creation of an atmosphere of confidence and mutual understanding" between the two countries.

Another Soviet objective—perhaps not recognized at the time—was the desire to gain recognition for their efforts to change a backward agricultural country into a modern industrial state and for their achievements in the arts, culture and science which they tout as achievements of a communist society.

The foreign travel provided by cultural agreements was also an attraction for a country which had been isolated from the rest of the world since the late 1930s. There was a huge pent-up demand for foreign travel among the Soviet intelligentsia. Professionals in all fields, including party and government officials, wanted to travel to the West, and Khrushchev himself visited the United States in 1959 in a well-publicized tour. Exchange agreements enable the Soviet authorities to carefully vent and control this demand for foreign travel.

Exchanges could also be used to earn foreign currency. The Soviets have a surplus of world class performing artists, and their conservatories and international music competitions produce a new crop each year. The Soviets soon learned that they could receive world class fees for these artists and thus provide the Soviet treasury with another source of much-needed hard currency.

Finally, there is the Soviet fascination with the United States, based on seeming similarities as well as deep differences between the two societies, a fascination which has been intensified by the anti-American propaganda of the Soviet media. Nothing attracts like forbidden fruit.

U.S. Objectives

The main U.S. objective was to open the Soviet Union to Western influences in order to change its foreign and domestic policies.

For the U.S. government, the policy was set forth in NSC 5607, "East-West Exchanges," a National Security Council statement of policy dated June 29, 1956.[11]

This document, couched in the Cold War rhetoric of the time, was to serve, without revision, as the basic U.S. government policy statement on East-West exchanges through the 1970s, and perhaps beyond.

It begins with the premise that U.S. policy is to promote evolutionary changes within the Soviet Union "toward a regime which will abandon predatory policies, . . . seek to promote the aspirations of the Russian people rather than the global ambitions of International Communism, and which will increasingly rest upon the consent of the governed . . ." As for the satellites, the document states that ". . . we seek their evolution toward independence of Moscow."

U.S. objectives, the document continues, are to increase the Soviet bloc's knowledge of the outer world so that their judgments are based on fact rather than "Communist fiction," to encourage freedom of thought, to stimulate the demand for greater personal security for bloc citizens, to encourage their desire for more consumer goods and to stimulate nationalism within the satellites in an effort to encourage "defiance of Moscow."

To achieve these noble objectives, the NSC statement lists the seventeen proposals presented by the three Western powers to the

Soviet Union at the 1955 Geneva Foreign Ministers meeting, and suggests that they be used as a general guide, with each proposal being judged on its own merits as to whether it contributes to the agreed objectives.

These proposals include, among others, the freer exchange of information and ideas; the distribution of official publications of each country in the other countries; exchanges of books, periodicals and newspapers; exchanges of films on a commercial basis; the exchange of exhibitions; an end to radio jamming and censorship of outgoing press despatches; access of journalists to normal sources of information; and the encouragement of tourism and exchanges of persons in the cultural, scientific and technical fields, including students and athletes.

U.S. private initiatives should be welcomed, the statement adds, when "they advance U.S. policy or seem to be an acceptable and necessary price for what will advance U.S. policy." This cavalier dismissal of the private sector in Soviet-American exchanges was a major misjudgment of the role which the private sector would increasingly play in these exchanges as they developed over the following years. Indeed, these exchanges would never have developed as they did, had it not been for the overwhelming approval of the U.S. public, the participation of the private sector in the exchanges and the support of the U.S. Congress.

Exchanges were welcomed in the United States at large as a means of learning more about the Soviet Union, an interest shared by both the government and the private sector. The Cold War had sparked an enormous interest in the Soviet Union, and this interest was fanned by Soviet secrecy about their internal affairs. Whatever the United States could learn about the Soviet Union was of interest, not only to the State Department and U.S. intelligence agencies, but also to American industry which saw the Soviet Union as a vast potential market as well as a possible competitor.

The scholarly community also had a high interest in learning more about the Soviet Union. A handful of American scholars had studied there in the early 1930s, and a few had served in our Moscow embassy during or immediately after World War II, but this was hardly enough to fill the needs of academia.[12] Between 1936 and 1958, no U.S. scholar had been able to study in the Soviet Union, a gap of twenty-two years in U.S. scholarship.

Soviet studies in the United States had been encouraged during World War II to meet the U.S. government's needs for specialists on our wartime ally. After the war, centers of Soviet studies were established at Columbia, Harvard and Berkeley, and at other major universities in the following years. The 1950s saw the start of Soviet studies as an academic discipline. Assisted by funding from the government and the foundations, it soon became a growth area. Here too there was a convergence of public and private interest, since the government needed the specialists which academia was producing.

The Inter-University Committee on Travel Grants (IUCTG) was established in 1956 to send American scholars to the Soviet Union as tourists on thirty-day visits, the only way they could travel there at that time. More than 200 Americans went to the Soviet Union under IUCTG auspices between 1956 and 1960. IUCTG wanted to send scholars on longer visits for study and research, but it was at first not interested in an exchange program with the Soviets. Moscow, however, sought similar opportunities for Soviet scholars and scientists in the United States, and due to this mutual interest a reciprocal exchange of U.S. and Soviet scholars began under the cultural agreement.

Private American citizens were also interested in travel to the Soviet Union. They had a curiosity about that vast country, similar to their interest in other parts of the world in the postwar era. As the English became known as world travelers in the heyday of the British Empire, the Americans became world tourists in the era of their country's superpower status.

And within the U.S. government there was the new United States Information Agency (USIA) whose mission, in the words of its motto, was to tell America's story to the world. USIA had a special interest in several of the seventeen points mentioned in NSC 5607, namely the freer exchange of information and ideas; opening of information centers; distribution of books, periodicals and newspapers; exchange of government publications, radio broadcasts and films; and an end to radio jamming. USIA, therefore, was to play a leading role in many of the exchanges under the cultural agreement.

Ambassador Lacy, in opening the cultural negotiations, described U.S. goals as "progress in removing barriers currently obstructing the free flow of information and ideas," and this was a continuing objective of all administrations over the years.[13] Lacy, citing the 1955 Geneva proposals, also called for periodic exchanges of radio and TV broadcasts on current events, and an end to Soviet censorship of reporting by foreign correspondents, jamming of radio broadcasts and controls over access to information and travel. Although not publicly stated at the time, it was also hoped that opening up the Soviet Union to Western influences would create pressures from within for reforms which might make the Soviet Union more likely to cooperate with, rather than confront, the West.

Khrushchev, in his memoirs, has summarized the U.S. objectives as seen by the Soviets:

The Americans wanted a much broader exchange of tourists, scientists and students. . . . Many of their suggestions were clearly intended to make us open our borders, to increase the flow of people back and forth.[14]

The Early Years (1958–1972)

The early years of exchanges were the learning years, when two vastly different societies had to learn how to work together. The watchwords on both sides were control, strict reciprocity and suspicion. It was a very frustrating and time consuming experience, but it served to establish procedures and patterns which, for better or worse, were to govern the future of these exchanges.

Months passed before many exchanges began, although they had been specified in the cultural agreement. It was one thing to agree on an exchange of delegations, but another to agree on the cities they would visit, what they would see in those cities, whether Embassy officers could accompany them, etc. Each side hesitated to make a concession without a reciprocal move from the other side.

And for the U.S. side, there was another issue to be resolved in each exchange, who would pay the costs, the U.S. government or the private sector organization carrying out the exchange.[15] In this respect, as in many others, the private sector was to become a much more important factor in exchanges than the drafters of NSC 5607 had anticipated.

In carrying out the agreed exchanges each side sought to maximize results for its primary objectives—for the Soviets, access to U.S. science and technology, and for the United States, the freer flow of people, ideas and information. To this end, American diplomats used whatever leverage they had, which often meant trading off Soviet interests in science and technology for U.S. interests in exchanges of people and information.

Mechanisms to control exchanges under the agreement were established early by both governments. In the Soviet Union, the central point for coordination was the State Committee for Cultural Relations with Foreign Countries, until 1967 when its functions were taken over by the Cultural Affairs Department of the Ministry of Foreign Affairs. In the United States, it was initially the East-West Contacts Staff in the Department of State, which in 1960 became the Soviet and Eastern European Exchanges Staff in State's Bureau of European Affairs.

The State Committee took a confrontational attitude on most exchanges, reflecting not only the Cold War attitude of the times but also the career affiliation of many of its officers—the KGB—and compensating, perhaps, for Soviet insecurity in doing business with the United States. The Americans reciprocated. It was strictly tit-for-tat.

Each proposal for an exchange was presented to the other government in the form of a diplomatic aide mémoire. This was very useful in avoiding misunderstandings—always possible in Soviet-American relations—but it considerably slowed the process of getting on with exchanges.

Security and intelligence were major considerations for both sides. Travel and access for exchange visitors were tightly controlled in each country.[16] While it was normal practice in the Soviet Union to close most of its territory to travel by foreigners and to limit their access to Soviet institutions and individuals, this was not normal practice in the United States. U.S. escorts, nevertheless, were provided for all Soviet exchange delegations which were held to prearranged itineraries from which they could not deviate without authorization from the State Department.

Travel restrictions were placed on long-term Soviet visitors, although they were exempted from the closed area procedures applicable to Soviet diplomats, journalists and trade representatives. Soviet scientists, scholars and students in residence at U.S. universities could not—and still cannot— travel beyond a twenty-five mile radius of their place of study without prior notification to the State Department. And prior approval was required if the visit was to another university or scientific facility. These U.S. restrictions were imposed in retaliation for a similar forty kilometer limit on travel by Americans in the Soviet Union. These procedures are still in effect in both countries.

Exchange visitors were under surveillance in both countries. Americans in the Soviet Union were often harassed and occasionally entrapped by the KGB. It was not unusual each year for one or more American exchange visitors to be expelled by the Soviet authorities for an alleged infringement of Soviet laws or regulations, or to be withdrawn by the U.S. side to avoid expulsion or entrapment. In such cases there was often a reciprocal expulsion of a Soviet visitor from the United States. This pattern of harassment and expulsion did not end until the early 1970s.

The number of persons exchanged annually by each side during the early years was not large initially. In 1958, the first year of official exchanges, 516 Soviets came to the United States under the agreement. The number had risen to about 1,000 by the mid-1960s, depending on how many symphony orchestras or track teams traveled in a particular year. With the 1964 agreement, in a Soviet reaction to the war in Vietnam, a downward trend began. An increase began with the 1970 agreement, as détente loomed on the horizon, and by 1972 the number had tripled, compared to 1958.[17] In any given year, the number of Soviets and Americans exchanged under the agreement were about the same.

Despite these difficulties, the early years produced many positive results. While not exactly normalizing relations, a dialogue began between professionals of the two countries in a wide variety of fields. Procedures were established—ground rules, which facilitated exchanges in all fields covered by the agreement. Each side learned how to work with the other, adapting to the peculiarities of the other country, its laws and traditions. And, as an indication of how highly each side values exchanges, they managed to survive the chill in bilateral relations brought on by the Vietnam War.

In retrospect, each government showed considerable flexibility in stretching its laws and traditions to accommodate the new exchanges. This could not have occurred without the cultural agreement, the approval of exchanges by the two governments at the highest level and, in the United States, broad support for the exchanges by the public and the Congress.

This first phase of Soviet-American exchanges might be described as exchange tourism, with each side sending its leading specialists for a look at what the other was doing. Exchange tourism set the stage for the second phase, cooperative activities, when bilateral relations had improved in the 1970s and the détente years began.

The Détente Years (1972–1979)

The 1970s brought many changes in U.S.-USSR relations. The Cold War was replaced by détente, and in exchanges, the learning years by years of cooperation.

At the Nixon-Brezhnev summit meetings of 1972, 1973 and 1974, scientific exchanges were spun off from the cultural agreement to eleven agreements for cooperation in various fields of science and technology. The motivation was mainly political, to broaden and deepen bilateral relations, to create an interlocking framework of obligations and incentives, to develop patterns and habits of cooperation in solving common problems and to end Soviet isolation and inward orientation.

On the Soviet side, exchanges were recognized as a legitimate element in bilateral relations. The Soviets became easier to work with. Younger and more professionally qualified people began to appear on Soviet delegations. Security considerations continued but were downplayed on both sides. The Soviets also got a psychological boost from the cooperative agreements. In their view, the Soviet Union had been formally recognized as coequal with the United States.

A new cultural agreement, signed at the 1973 summit, was valid for six years rather than the previous two, implying more continuity and permanence to exchanges. The Soviets had suggested a five-year agreement but U.S. negotiators balked at a joint Soviet-American five-year plan for exchanges. But the agreement, after the spinoff of science and technology, was left with only culture, education, information, sports, tourism and what subsequently became known as "public diplomacy." The leverage which the United States formerly had, in trading off exchanges in science and technology for those in culture and education, had been lost.

The State Department initially had opposed the spinoff of science and technology from the cultural agreement, preferring to retain all exchanges under a general agreement in order to maintain a degree of leverage in its negotiations with the Soviets. When it was overruled, State, as a last resort, recommended that all of the cooperative agreements include, in their preamble, a reference to the general agreement which would serve as the "umbrella" agreement for exchanges, and to which the cooperative agreements would be subsidiary. This suggestion was adopted when the first cooperative agreement, on environmental protection, was negotiated, and all the others followed the same procedure. Since 1973, as a consequence, the cultural agreements have all contained, up front, a listing of the cooperative agreements.

Exchanges in all fields increased greatly during détente. By 1977, the number of Soviet visitors to the United States under all exchange programs—including the eleven cooperative agreements—had grown to 4,615, including 1,060 tourists, or half of all Soviet citizens who received U.S. visas in that fiscal year. The increase was so great that the State Department, in the mid-1970s, ceased publication of its semiannual reports which, since the beginning of official exchanges, had listed all exchanges conducted under the cultural agreement.[18]

In education, the Soviets agreed to new exchanges of university lecturers and graduate students in the arts, as well as direct exchanges between U.S. and Soviet universities.

The exchange of scholars expanded, and a new agreement between the American Council of Learned Societies and the Soviet Academy of Sciences for cooperative research in the social sciences and humanities was signed in 1975. This agreement met a longstanding U.S. objective of collaborative research in these fields.

The Soviets in the 1970s also discovered the U.S. private sector. During the Nixon and Ford administrations, State's Bureau of

Educational and Cultural Affairs, under Assistant Secretary John Richardson, was actively encouraging U.S. private sector organizations to become involved in international exchanges, and assisting them, as necessary, with grants of "seed" money. This policy was extended to Soviet exchanges, and many U.S. private organizations, with encouragement from State, began direct exchanges with their Soviet counterparts.

Among these were the YMCA International Division, National 4-H Foundation, American Library Association, American Bar Association, League of Women Voters, National Governors Association, U.S. Conference of Mayors, American Council of Young Political Leaders and several regional theaters.

In an effort to move beyond the exchange tourism of the early years of exchanges, bilateral seminars were held to help each side understand the workings of the other in such fields as education, publishing, library science, law, literature and theater.

Cultural exchanges were released from the strictures of the intergovernmental agreement with its quotas and limits. The private sector was invited by State to participate in what previously had been a government-directed and regulated activity, and the result was a broadening of U.S. contracts with the Soviet Union.

The central control of exchanges within each government was relaxed somewhat. In the State Department, the Soviet and Eastern European Exchanges Staff gave up its operational responsibilities for exchanges to the Bureau of Educational and Cultural Affairs, retaining only its policy function. More important, it became possible for U.S. private organizations to deal directly with their Soviet counterparts.

This Soviet discovery of the U.S. private sector—many years after the East Europeans had discovered it and learned how to work with it—gave the Soviets the best of two worlds. They were able to work directly with U.S. private organizations which, in many cases, did not have very much expertise on the Soviet Union initially and were therefore more receptive to Soviet suggestions on how to conduct the exchanges. At the same time, the Soviets were able to conduct these exchanges under the protective cover of the intergovernmental agreement. In the process, the American exchange partners, after a few years, learned how to work with the Soviets.

The Soviets, earlier, in 1967, had dissolved the State Committee for Cultural Relations with Foreign Countries. In its place, a new Department of Cultural Relations was established in the Ministry of Foreign Affairs which had a greater interest than the Committee in expanding exchanges with the West. The day-to-day conduct of exchanges was delegated to Soviet ministries and institutions, each of which, however, had a foreign department which exercised political control, and was often staffed by KGB personnel. Nevertheless, another small step forward had been taken in normalizing cultural relations.

The Soviet invasion of Afghanistan, in December 1979, brought a suspension of many of the exchanges conducted by the two governments. Other exchanges continued, however, because of the increasingly larger role played by U.S. private organizations, many of which decided to continue their exchanges with the Soviets despite the U.S. government suspension.

Indeed, what had begun in 1958 as a joint effort by the U.S. government and the private sector, had evolved into a largely private sector program.

Notes

1. *United States Treaties and Other International Agreements* (hereafter *TIAS*) 3975, vol. 9, 1958, pp. 13–39.

2. *TIAS* 4362, vol. 10, pt. 2, 1959, pp. 1934–1977.

3. *TIAS* 5112, vol. 13, pt. 2, 1962, pp. 1496–1562.

4. *TIAS* 7649, vol. 24, pt. 2, 1973, pp. 1395–1438.

5. A *TIAS* number is not expected to be assigned to the 1985 agreement until some time in 1987. The text of the agreement is appended to this study as Appendix B.

6. Robert F. Byrnes, *Soviet-American Academic Exchanges, 1958–1975* (Bloomington: Indiana University Press, 1976), pp. 30–31.

7. For the text of the seventeen points, see Appendix A.

8. *New York Times*, November 15, 1955, p. 10.

9. Ibid.

10. *Department of State Bulletin*, November 18, 1957, p. 802.

11. The full text of NSC 5607 is appended as Appendix A.

12. See Byrnes, pp. 17–30, for the origins and development of Soviet area studies in the United States.

13. *Department of State Bulletin*, November 18, 1957, pp. 800–801.

14. Strobe Talbott (ed. & tr.), *Khrushchev Remembers: The Last Testament* (Boston: Little, Brown and Co., 1974), p. 409.

15. The term "side" (*storona* in Russian), as distinguished from "government," has been used, in exchange jargon, to indicate that the U.S. partner in exchanges conducted under the intergovernmental agreement may be either the U.S. government or the private sector.

16. "Access" is the term used in exchanges to indicate access to scholarly sources, as in the case of scholars conducting research, or to officials and other sources of information, as in the case of journalists.

17. These figures and much other useful data on exchanges are taken from "Survey of U.S. Educational and Cultural Exchanges with the Soviet Union and

Eastern Europe," a classified report prepared for the State Department by Boris H. Klosson on June 23, 1978, and declassified and released under the Freedom of Information Act on December 24, 1984. Mr. Klosson was Director of the Soviet and Eastern European Exchanges Staff from 1965 to 1969.

18. *Report on Exchanges with the Soviet Union and Eastern Europe,* prepared by the Soviet and Eastern European Exchanges Staff, Department of State, and published semi-annually (Washington, D.C.: U.S. Government Printing Office).

2

Performing Arts

The most visible of all Soviet-American exchanges have been in the performing arts, a world of ballet dancers, symphony orchestras, virtuoso soloists, folk dancers, theater, ice shows, circuses and jazz. It is also a strange mix of the arts, publicity and lucrative, but risky, business. And with the Soviets involved, it also becomes political.

Americans are aware of the impact made in the United States by the Bolshoi Ballet, the Moiseyev Dance Ensemble, the Soviet symphony orchestras and virtuoso soloists. But most Americans cannot begin to appreciate the impact made in the Soviet Union by the New York City Ballet, American Ballet Theater, Alvin Ailey Dance Theater, Paul Taylor Dance Company, Benny Goodman, Duke Ellington, Preservation Hall Jazz Band, Arena Stage, American Conservatory Theater and Jessica Tandy and Hume Cronyn in the Pulitzer Prize-winning play, "The Gin Game," to name a few of the ensembles that went to the Soviet Union between the late 1950s and the end of 1979 under these reciprocal exchanges.

To Soviet audiences, isolated from Western cultural influences since the 1930s, the visits by American and other Western artists brought a breath of fresh air as well as new artistic concepts in music, dance and theater to a country where orthodoxy and conservatism have long ruled in the performing arts.

Countries conduct cultural exchanges to show off their achievements and to generate good will. For the United States, however, cultural exchanges with the Soviet Union have also been used to break down barriers to a freer exchange of people, ideas and information. Cultural exchanges have brought new art forms to the Soviet Union—modern dance, jazz, blues and country music— and demonstrate American pre-eminence in the arts. And cultural officers of the American Embassy in Moscow use the presence of the visiting American artists to arrange workshops, master classes, demonstrations, joint rehearsals and, in the case of jazz, jam sessions with Soviet artists as well as free performances for conservatory students.

For the Soviet Union, cultural exchanges provide an opportunity to demonstrate its achievements in music, dance and theater—of which it is justly proud. Foreign tours also gratify some of the pent-up desire of the Soviet cultural intelligentsia for travel abroad and the stimulation provided by interchange with other cultures. There is also a financial incentive for the artists. Soviet artists do not earn much, if anything, while abroad, but the tours provide an opportunity to purchase Western goods for resale at home on the black market at a substantial profit, a practice which has been well documented by Galina Vishnevskaya.[1]

There is also a political payoff. Soviet artists project an image of a vital, talented and creative people whose government suppports the arts and is dedicated to peace and friendship with all countries. If you like the Bolshoi, this line of thought goes, you might also like the Bolsheviks. In this regard, however, Soviet propaganda overlooks the fact that what they send abroad—in ballet, music, folk dance and theater—is largely a legacy of Russia's tsarist past and its national traditions.

Ideology also plays a role. Cultural exchanges are seen by the Soviets as another aspect of the competition between communist and capitalist societies in which the stronger must triumph.

The financial factor, however, is the bottom line for the Soviets, both abroad and at home. Performing artists on tour abroad earn hard currency for the Soviet state, and in recent years the Soviet Union has been very active in mining this bonanza. And tours by American artists in the Soviet Union are usually sold out and show a profit in rubles.

Arts exchanges are not easy to administer. Two very different systems of arts management have to work together, one controlled by the state, and the other by the free market, under an agreement between the two governments which determines both the number and the art forms of the artists to be exchanged. The result, in the United States, has been a curious mix of government and private sector activity which has characterized so many Soviet-American exchanges.

Soviet artists perform abroad under the auspices of the USSR State Concert Agency—Goskontsert in Soviet parlance—a state monopoly which functions as a foreign trade organization under control of the USSR Ministry of Culture. Tours in the United States for Soviet artists are arranged by Goskontsert under contracts negotiated by Goskontsert directly with the U.S. concert agencies on a commercial basis. Hurok Concerts, founded by the legendary Sol Hurok, and Columbia Artists

Management were the pioneers among U.S. concert agencies in arranging these tours but many others have entered the field in recent years.

Soviet performers were an instant box office success in the United States, and many were booked on extensive coast-to-coast tours for as long as two to three months, with side trips to Canada and Mexico. Impresarios are reluctant to discuss the financial terms of their very competitive business, but the fees paid for Soviet artists are believed to be substantial. (The going rate these days for a major symphony orchestra ranges from $10,000 to $20,000 or more a performance; for a prominent soloist or conductor it can be about $5,000.)

In the early years of exchanges a substantial portion of the fees is believed to have gone to the Soviet artists, but this soon changed and the bulk of the proceeds now go to the Soviet government, with the soloists receiving only a modest amount.[2] Whatever other reasons the Soviets may have had for these exchanges, the earning of hard currency soon became a major objective, and Goskontsert learned to play off one foreign impresario against another to obtain the highest possible fee.

Estimates vary for the annual dollar earnings of the Soviet government for the performing artists it sends to the United States. One informed estimate in 1978 put the yearly earnings between $300,000 and $1,000,000.[3] Furthermore, the fees paid by the U.S. impresarios are remitted, not to Moscow but to the Soviet Embassy in Washington where they are used to pay Embassy costs, and perhaps the costs of Soviet espionage activities in the United States, as Vishnevskaya charges.[4]

The United States, by contrast, has had to deal with a state monopoly in order to book reciprocal tours by American artists in the Soviet Union. Goskontsert does not pay world-class fees for foreign artists, and what it does pay is usually a combination of dollars and rubles—short on the dollars and long on the rubles which are non-convertible in the Soviet Union and cannot be exported legally. American artists fill halls in the Soviet Union and they guarantee a profit in rubles. This is one reason they are welcome in the Soviet Union, if the price is right.

American performers, however, usually have no great interest in performing in the Soviet Union unless someone pays their customary fees in hard currency, and this is where the U.S. government has had to step in with a subsidy. The State Department's Bureau of Educational and Cultural Affairs—a part of USIA since 1978—selected the American performers and proposed them to Goskontsert through the American Embassy in Moscow. Acceptance by Goskontsert, however, was not always assured. The Soviets often insisted on reviewing artistic ensembles in performance before final acceptance. Some U.S. ensembles, particularly those that were considered by the Soviets as too avant garde or not in accord with Soviet ideology—some jazz bands for example—were not accepted. Once approval had been given, the American Embassy in Moscow signed a contract with Goskontsert specifying the financial and other terms of the tour.

Negotiation of contracts was always difficult and lengthy, with the Americans trying to maximize the impact of the tours and the portion of the fees paid in dollars. In all cases, however, there was a net financial loss to the U.S. government.

The dollar fee paid by Goskontsert for U.S. artists was minimal. Moreover, the State Department had to sign contracts with the American artists and pay them a dollar fee, using funds appropriated by the Congress for international cultural exchanges. Thus, while the Soviet Union earned much-needed dollars for the artists it sent to the United States, the U.S. government has had to subsidize, in dollars, the Americans it sent to the Soviet Union in exchange. The dollars paid by the Soviets reverted to the U.S. Treasury, while the rubles were retained by the American Embassy in Moscow to cover some of its local expenses.

A catch-22 situation developed in 1979 when the Soviets denied the Embassy the right to use these rubles, which therefore could be neither converted, nor exported nor used within the Soviet Union, and it is a violation of Soviet law to destroy them. This issue was never formally resolved, but the Soviets must have realized the absurdity of their position because they agreed, later in 1979, to pay the full, although substandard, fee in dollars for "The Gin Game," the play starring Jessica Tandy and Hume Cronyn. This was the last U.S. performing arts ensemble in the Soviet Union under the cultural agreement before it expired at the end of 1979.

Itineraries of the American artists in the Soviet Union were often contested. All Americans in the Soviet Union, including visiting artists, are limited to those areas which are open to travel by foreigners. In the early years of exchanges this meant only the European parts of the Soviet Union—usually Moscow, Leningrad, Kiev and a few other cities. Efforts to broaden the itineraries to include cities where there was far less contact with the West were met by Soviet excuses, sometimes justified, that there were no suitable concert halls or hotel accommodations in those cities, or that the cities were located in closed areas.

Soviet exchange visitors to the United States, by contrast, are exempted from the travel restrictions imposed by the U.S. government on Soviet officials, journalists and trade representatives. Soviet artists, consequently, perform all over the United States.

Other difficulties beset these exchanges. American artists initially were flattered by invitations from the State Department to perform in the Soviet Union. This interest waned with time, however, as artists were turned off by the poor accommodations and services in the Soviet Union, Soviet insistence in reviewing their programs in advance and Soviet human rights violations.

The limited funds available to the State Department determined both the quality and the type of artists it could send abroad. State normally had about one million dollars a year for its performing arts exchanges worldwide, and in a typical year about half this amount would be spent in the Soviet Union and Eastern Europe. Since a symphony orchestra or dance company could cost $200,000 or more for a two-week tour in the 1970s—and much more in the 1980s when USIA has about the same amount of funds available—this did not leave sufficient funds for other ensembles.

To get around its funding problem, State would often seek artists who did not require a dollar fee, such as university or conservatory ensembles. While these were of high artistic quality, the Soviets did not consider them an adequate exchange for the prestigious ensembles they were sending to the United States. In this regard, USIA was very fortunate in 1986 in getting the world-renowned pianist Vladimir Horowitz, who performed in the Soviet Union without a fee, as the first American artist under the 1985 agreement.

The number of ensembles exchanged under the cultural agreement was small at the start—three from each country over the two years covered by each cultural agreement—but by 1972 the number had increased to six. With détente and pressures from both the Soviets and U.S. impresarios to increase exchanges, the 1973 agreement provided for the exchange of "at least ten" performing arts groups and "at least thirty-five" individual artists over a three-year period. (The numbers in the 1985 agreement are "at least" ten and ten, respectively.) Since the number of American groups which could be sent to the Soviet Union was limited by the funds appropriated by Congress—the same one million dollars—this, in effect, allowed the Soviets to send as many artists as the U.S. market could absorb, while the United States was limited to two or three ensembles in the Soviet Union each year.

The Soviets took full advantage of this opportunity. During the 1978–1979 concert year—the last before the cultural agreement lapsed—they sent ten ensembles and thirty individual artists, whereas the United States was not able to send more than two ensembles during the same period. The hard currency earnings for the Soviet treasury are believed to have been considerable.

Security for Soviet performers in the United States was a major concern of both governments. Demonstrations against Soviet performers were staged by American groups opposed to exchanges with the Soviet Union. The harassment became more widespread and often violent in the 1970s with protests by the militant Jewish Defense League against Soviet emigration policy. A 1970 U.S. tour by the Bolshoi Ballet was cancelled by the Soviets for this reason. The Soviet government repeatedly sought assurances of security for its artists, but the State Department could only respond that it would do everything within its power. This usually meant asking local authorities to take necessary measures to protect the Soviet artists and to prevent disruptions of their performances, measures that were sometimes inadequate and did not always deter violence.

Defections by Soviet artists became another problem as more and more of them traveled abroad. In the early years of exchanges, the defections of dancers Rudolf Nureyev (1961 in Paris), Natalya Makarova (1970 in London) and Mikhail Baryshnikov (1974 in Toronto) did not interrupt Soviet exchanges with the West. Soviet pride was hurt by the loss of these and other Soviet artists, but their defections were separated by intervals of several years which somewhat cushioned the shock.

But during a Bolshoi Ballet tour of the United States in 1979, there were defections by dancers Aleksander Godunov (August 22) and Valentina and Leonid Kozlov (September 16). Godunov's defection was followed by a nasty standoff between the two governments at New York's Kennedy airport when U.S. officials refused to permit the departure of his wife, Bolshoi dancer Lyudmila Vlasova, until they could determine whether she was leaving the United States voluntarily.

To climax a bad month for Soviet exchanges, the Soviet Olympic and World Championship Pairs Skating team of Lyudmila Belousova and Oleg Protopopov defected in Switzerland on September 22.

Soviet reaction was swift. On September 27, the Soviets cancelled a U.S. tour by the USSR State Symphony which was to have begun on October 4. The Soviets had unsuccessfully sought from the U.S. impresario "guarantees of security" for members of the orchestra, a euphemism for guarantee against defection. Also cancelled was a U.S. tour by two dancers from the Bolshoi.

The Soviet demand for "guarantees of security" was to arise again in December 1979 when it proved to be an obstacle to renewal of the cultural agreement. And when the cultural agreement lapsed at the end of December and Jimmy Carter imposed sanctions in response to the Soviet invasion of Afghanistan, the Soviets cancelled their entire season in the United States.

Mstislav Rostropovich has said that Soviet artists would not defect if they could easily leave the Soviet Union. The director of Washington's National Symphony Orchestra explained:

> They would simply travel to make more money. If they could negotiate their own contracts, pay their own taxes and were free to come and go, instead of being shackled and nursemaided and watched everywhere they went abroad, I'm sure there would be no reason for defections.[5]

The first Russian defections to the West, as historians like to point out, occurred during the reign of Tsar Boris Godunov in the late sixteenth century. Tsar Boris, an early Westernizer, selected thirty future leaders of Russia and sent them abroad to study in the West. Only two returned to Russia.[6]

Defections have always troubled Soviet officials, as well as Russian tsars. The defector, like the citizen who applies to emigrate, is seen as having rejected Soviet society and is considered a traitor. Some Soviet cultural officials recognize that creative artists need to travel abroad, but these same officials are reluctant to permit their artists to travel freely. When I once asked a senior Ministry of Culture official why his government did not permit its artists to reside abroad for lengthy periods as the East European governments do, he angrily replied, "Because they are Soviet artists." So much for the universality of art.

Meanwhile the defections of world-renowned Soviet artists continue—conductors Kiril Kondrashin and Maksim Shostakovich, theater director Yuri Lyubimov, film director Andrei Tarkovsky and others—and there is some evidence in 1986 that the Soviets may be modifying their opposition to residence abroad for Soviet artists. A few privileged Soviet artists, it is reported, are now permitted to reside in the West and to perform there in exchange for a percentage of their earnings being paid to the Soviet state.

In any event, as regards defecting artists, the Soviet loss is the West's gain.

The Soviet invasion of Afghanistan in December 1979 and the lapse of the cultural agreement at the end of 1979 brought a suspension of performing arts exchanges between the two countries. This suspension was to last until January 1986, when the Empire State Institute for the Performing Arts, a professional theater from Albany, New York, performed the children's musical, "Rag Dolly," at Moscow's Children's Musical Theater. This signaled the resumption of performing arts exchanges under the new cultural agreement which had been signed at the Reagan-Gorbachev Geneva summit less than two months earlier.

In conclusion, the performing arts, once considered to be the least controversial of all exchanges with the Soviet Union, have turned out to be as political and as difficult as most of the other exchanges which will be discussed in this study.

Notes

1. Galina Vishnevskaya, *Galina, A Russian Story* (New York: Harcourt Brace Jovanovich), pp. 296–297.
2. Ibid., p. 295.
3. Boris H. Klossen, "Survey of U.S. Educational and Cultural Exchanges with the Soviet Union and Eastern Europe," a classified report prepared by Boris H. Klosson for the Department of State on June 23, 1978, and declassified and released under the Freedom of Information Act on December 24, 1984, p. 112.
4. Vishnevskaya, p. 295.
5. *Washington Post*, April 27, 1983, p. 83.
6. Hans von Eckhardt, *Ivan the Terrible* (New York: Knopf, 1949), p. 49.

3

Exhibitions

Introduction

Exhibition exchange is another high visibility activity under the cultural agreement. Soviet and U.S. exhibitions are seen in major cities of the two countries by large numbers of people, and they tell each country something about the other.

There are two types—information exhibitions, mounted by the two governments and designed to present information about the sponsoring country, and art exhibitions, mounted by the museums of the two countries.

Governmental exhibitions have been a recurring and controversial feature of the cultural agreement since its inception. Called "thematic" exhibitions, they are built around a particular theme and are designed to demonstrate the achievements of the country—for the United States, its high standard of living, the products of its consumer society and, indirectly, the benefits of its market economy and democratic form of government; for the Soviet Union, the achievements of communism in transforming a backward country into a superpower.

The exchange of art exhibitions between museums began in the 1970s during the détente years, the result of efforts by major U.S. museums, such as New York's Metropolitan Museum, Washington's National Gallery of Art and private citizens such as Armand Hammer, to show the treasures of Soviet museums in the United States. Although the U.S. government is not a party to these exchanges, they take place, nevertheless, under a provision of the cultural agreement, added in 1970, which commits the two governments to render assistance to the exchange of exhibitions between museums of the two countries. This language, in effect, gives the blessings of the two governments to these private exchanges—private at least on the U.S. side.

Governmental Exhibitions

Exhibition exchanges began with national exhibitions in Moscow and Washington in 1959 under the first cultural agreement. These exhibitions were designed to show the best each country had to offer in a wide variety of fields. It was at the Moscow exhibition that then Vice President Richard M. Nixon held his highly publicized "kitchen debate" with Nikita Khrushchev. Each subsequent cultural agreement provided for additional exhibitions, usually one each year, until 1979 when the cultural agreement lapsed and the exchange was suspended.

The U.S. thematic exhibitions have been mounted by USIA which has responsibility for U.S. government exhibitions abroad. The USIA exhibitions have had a phenomenal success in the Soviet Union, and the Soviet authorities probably wished they had never agreed to accept them, for they have attempted several times to delete them from the cultural agreement. The titles of the U.S. exhibitions shown between 1960 and 1979 explain why: Plastics, Transportation, Medicine, Technical Books, Graphic Arts, Communications, Architecture, Hand Tools, Industrial Design, Education, Research and Development, Outdoor Recreation, Technology for the American Home, Photography, USA—200 Years (a bicentennial exhibition) and Agriculture. Designed to show the latest developments in these fields, they were graphic evidence of how far the Soviet Union lagged behind the United States.

Each USIA exhibition was shown for one month each in three Soviet cities until 1969 when, for reasons of economy, their tours were extended to six cities. Total attendance for all U.S. exhibitions is 16.8 million, averaging 250,000 in each city.

The exhibitions were an eyeopener for the Soviet public. They showed products never before seen in the Soviet Union, and they were very attractive to the eye, with their art work, color and methods of display. They also showed how technology can raise the standard of living of the average citizen. Each exhibition included a collection of books and periodicals on the subject theme, and American experts assigned to the exhibition staff conducted workshops for invited Soviet specialists.

Twenty young Americans, speaking Russian, served as guides for each exhibition. Stationed at various displays, they explained them to the Soviet visitors and answered questions about the products shown and about the United States in general. These were the first Americans most Soviets had ever seen, and they could converse with them in Russian. Soviet public response was very enthusiastic, and the guides were thronged by inquisitive Soviet citizens eager to satisfy their curiosity about the United States.

As Soviet public interest mounted, so did the concern of the Soviet authorities over this U.S. attempt to endrun their control of information about the United States, and various forms of harassment were used to limit the effectiveness of the exhibitions.

The Soviet authorities, always apprehensive about crowds, assigned "crowd controllers" to the long lines—usually several city blocks long—awaiting entry to the exhibitions. Hecklers were assigned to challenge and dispute statements by the American guides and to disrupt their conversations with Soviet visitors. Various subterfuges were used to make it difficult for Soviet citizens to visit the exhibitions—their location, opening and closing hours, and the number of days they were open. And when relations cooled between the two countries during the Vietnam War, there were nasty incidents of harassment staged against the exhibitions and their U.S. personnel.

On the diplomatic front, the Soviets, during the negotiation of each cultural agreement, sought to whittle down the number of exhibitions to be exchanged, to delay their openings, and to limit their stays in the Soviet Union. The exhibition section of the agreement was usually the most difficult to reach agreement on and was customarily left to the end of the negotiation and the final tradeoffs when all other sections had been agreed to.

These difficulties continued even into the détente years. In negotiating the 1972–1973 agreement, for example, the Soviets sought to delete the exhibition exchange. The impasse was resolved in the U.S. favor only after American Ambassador Jacob D. Beam personally took the issue to Foreign Minister Andrei Gromyko. Throughout the years, the USIA and State Department position on exhibitions have been consistent—no cultural agreement unless it includes thematic exhibitions.

If the Soviets could not force an end to the exhibition exchange they have forced the U.S. government to pay exorbitant costs for them. The Soviets pay in dollars for their thematic exhibitions in the United States, including costs for halls, shipping and staff support. The Soviet exhibitions, however, have not been crowd pleasers. Although built around themes similar to those of the U.S. exhibitions, they are poorly designed, generally dull, and attendance has been disappointing to the Soviets. The USSR Chamber of Commerce, which has the responsibility for Soviet exhibitions abroad, consequently has sought to cut its losses on the exchange. One way to do this is to make it increasingly expensive for USIA to show its exhibitions in the Soviet Union.

By the curious illogic that often governs U.S.-USSR exchanges, USIA also pays in dollars for its exhibitions in the Soviet Union, and the Chamber of Commerce makes certain that it pays well. To the U.S. bill they add all possible charges, at exorbitant prices at the official exchange rate, requiring even payment of the salary and expenses of the Soviet official who accompanies each USIA exhibition. This official is supposed to assist the U.S. staff and to smooth the way with local Soviet authorities, and he does this when U.S.-USSR relations are good. But when relations are not good, this official often becomes an obstacle to U.S. efforts to maximize the effectiveness of its exhibitions. By contrast, the U.S. government has paid the salaries and expenses of U.S. officials it has assigned to Soviet exhibitions in the United States, and these officials have been of genuine assistance.

Museum Exchanges

Soviet disillusionment with the thematic exhibitions led, in part, to their interest in exchanges between museums of the two countries. The Soviet intent was to delete the thematic exhibitions from the cultural agreement and to replace them with art exhibitions which create fewer political problems. Art exhibitions also had a strong proponent in Yekaterina A. Furtseva, USSR Minister of Culture from 1960 to 1974, who was a strong supporter of Soviet cultural activities abroad.

Soviet museum holdings include priceless treasures from Western Europe as well as Russia, a legacy from the holdings of private Russian collectors before the 1917 revolution, treasures which any Western museum would be delighted to own. But efforts by U.S. and other Western museums to borrow Soviet-held art objects had been rebuffed by Soviet authorities for many years because of the risk of judicial seizure abroad to satisfy legal claims against the Soviet government. For this reason, the Soviets insisted that all private exhibition exchanges be considered as falling under the provisions of the cultural agreement, thereby assuring U.S. government protection. When the USSR Ministry of Culture tested the waters in lending its first painting to a U.S. museum in the early 1970s, it required first a letter from the State Department placing the loan under the protection of the cultural agreement.

Soviet fear of judicial seizure in the United States abated only after the granting by statute of immunity from the judicial process. Under this statute—22 U.S.C. 2459—foreign art objects in the United States may be granted immunity from the judicial process if they are of cultural significance and if the Secretary of State finds that their exhibition in the United States is in the national interest. With rare exceptions, this has been granted routinely.[1]

With this obstacle out of the way, the Soviets in 1975 signed a five-year agreement with New York's Metropolitan Museum for an exchange of five American and five Soviet exhibitions. Exchanges with the National Gallery of Art and other U.S. museums soon followed. The Soviets had discovered the private sector in exhibition exchanges and found it easier to work with than the U.S. government.

A suspension of the exhibition exchange—both governmental as well as private—came after the Soviet invasion of Afghanistan in December 1979 and lapse of the cultural agreement.

The first casualty of these events was a major Soviet exhibition, "Art from the Hermitage Museum of Leningrad," organized by the Minneapolis Art Institute and the Control Data Corporation, the Minneapolis computer firm which had signed an agreement with the Soviets to underwrite most of the costs. The exhibition was to open at the National Gallery of Art in Washington in May 1980 and then go on to four other U.S. cities. The Carter administration, however, as one of its sanctions against the Soviet Union for the invasion of Afghanistan, refused to authorize a finding that the exhibition was in the national interest, and immunity from the judicial process was therefore not granted. Without such immunity, the Ministry of Culture refused to send the exhibition which was valued at more than one million dollars.

Although no exhibitions were exchanged between the two countries from 1980 through 1985, contacts between Soviet and U.S. museums continued. Visits by museum directors were made, materials were exchanged and courtesies extended. Both sides were pleased with past exchanges and were willing to wait until an improvement in relations between the two governments would permit a resumption of their exchanges.

This occurred when a new cultural agreement was signed at the Reagan-Gorbachev Geneva summit in November 1985. The first major event under the new agreement was the opening in Leningrad on February 3, 1986, less than two months after the agreement had been signed, of an exhibition of forty French impressionist paintings from the National Gallery of Art. Exhibitions of this scope are usually planned two or more years in advance, and it was obvious, in this case, that the museum directors involved were also good political forecasters.

Notes

1. 22 U.S.C. 2459.

4

Scholars and Students

Introduction

Let's exchange 10,000 students with the Soviet Union. Such a proposal was made by President Eisenhower in 1958, and it has been repeated periodically by other prominent Americans over the years.[1]

Student exchange usually comes to mind when governments discuss cultural exchanges and seek ways to improve mutual understanding. And considering how much mutual understanding is needed between the United States and the Soviet Union, it is understandable that Americans should propose a big round number. But student exchanges, while seemingly noncontroversial, become another complex and difficult issue when placed on the agenda of U.S.-USSR relations.

Let's define the term—always a useful first step in dealing with the Soviets where words often seem to have other meanings. Americans use the word "student" loosely to describe anyone from a high school student to a graduate student. For the Soviets, however, as for most Europeans, a student is someone enrolled at a university-level institution, and they have other terms for high school and graduate students.

When the Soviets talk of student exchanges, what they have in mind, with rare exceptions, are scholars or scientists in their early or mid-thirties who have completed their formal studies and are engaged in what the Russians call "scientific research." As for high school exchange, the Soviet response to such proposals for a school year abroad and living with a host family has always been "nyet." In a society which is trying to create a new Soviet man and which fears the competing attractions of the West on its youth, students are not to be sent abroad during their most impressionable years.

After twenty-eight years of Soviet-American cultural exchanges, the number of students, teachers and scholars exchanged in academic year 1985–1986 is still very small, about 600 Americans and 250 Soviets. To put these numbers into perspective, they should be contrasted with students from other countries who study in the United States each year. In academic year 1983–1984, for example, there were 13,010 from Japan, 5,860 from the United Kingdom, 3,790 from the Federal Republic of Germany, 3,150 from France and 10,000 from the People's Republic of China.[2]

The Programs

Heading the list of scholarly exchanges are the six programs conducted by the International Research and Exchanges Board (IREX), a New York-based organization established in 1968 at the request of the American Council of Learned Societies (ACLS) and the Social Science Research Council (SSRC) to administer academic exchanges with the Soviet Union and Eastern Europe. IREX is the successor to the Inter-University Committee on Travel Grants (IUCTG), which administered these scholarly exchanges from 1958 to 1968.

Three IREX programs are conducted with the USSR Ministry of Higher and Specialized Secondary Education (the Ministry). These are the Graduate Student/Young Faculty Exchange (hereinafter called Graduate Students) which normally exchanges about forty Americans and an equal number of Soviets for one or two semesters each year; Senior Research Scholars—ten or more professors on each side to conduct research for periods of two to five months; and thirty American teachers of Russian and an equal number of Soviet teachers of English for nine weeks each summer.

IREX also administers, on behalf of ACLS, an exchange of scholars for postdoctoral research in the social sciences and humanities with the Soviet Academy of Sciences—up to sixty person-months a year on each side, for some fifteen Americans and thirty Soviets, who come for shorter visits. In addition, IREX administers a program of collaborative research, conferences and workshops between ACLS and the Soviet Academy under their bilateral Commission on the Social Sciences and Humanities, established in 1975. About eighty Americans and eighty Soviets are exchanged each year under Commission activities, usually for visits of about one week. Between 1958 and the end of 1985, some 2,000 Americans and 2,000 Soviets were exchanged under IUCTG and IREX programs.

The three IREX-Ministry exchanges are considered by the two governments to be official programs under the cultural agreement.

These exchanges have been negotiated by the State Department—and by USIA since 1985—and the terms under which they take place are spelled out in the cultural agreement. The U.S. government, moreover, is the major funder of these exchanges, with grants to IREX from USIA, the Department of State (Title VIII, Soviet and East European Research and Training Program) and the National Endowment for the Humanities.

The ACLS exchange with the Soviet Academy, although also mentioned in the cultural agreement, has a less official status since both ACLS and the Soviet Academy are nongovernmental organizations. The ACLS–Soviet Academy Commission, a more recent arrival on the exchange scene, is not mentioned in the cultural agreement and is clearly a private program.

An exchange of university lecturers for periods of one to ten months each is conducted under the Fulbright Program, with "at least" fifteen persons to be exchanged annually from each side in all disciplines to lecture and to conduct research. This exchange is administered on the U.S. side by the Council for International Exchange of Scholars (CIES), and on the Soviet side by the Ministry.

Another Fulbright exchange—for five graduate students or young specialists each year in dance, music, theater, film, and the graphic and plastic arts—was suspended in 1980 by the USSR Ministry of Culture and was not reinstated when the new cultural agreement was signed in 1985, reportedly because the Ministry was no longer interested in sending young Soviet artists to the United States.

Private academic exchanges with the Soviet Union expanded during the détente years when U.S. universities and organizations, with encouragement from the State Department, began direct exchanges with Soviet academic institutions. These programs, although not mentioned in the cultural agreement, are considered by both governments as falling under the provision of the agreement which commits both governments to encourage and facilitate contacts, exchanges and cooperation in various fields of education.

The State University of New York (SUNY) conducts reciprocal exchanges with two Moscow institutions. With the Maurice Thorez Institute of Foreign Languages, SUNY, since 1974, has exchanged ten undergraduates and one faculty adviser in Russian and English language studies for one semester each year. The Soviet students, who are studying to be interpreters, are the only Soviet undergraduates who study in the United States, and the fact that they come as a group and are accompanied by a faculty member from their institute, speaks for the Soviet attitude on undergraduate exchanges.

With Moscow State University, SUNY has conducted, since 1976, a direct exchange of graduate students and faculty members in all academic disciplines. Ten to twelve graduate students and one faculty adviser from each university are exchanged each year, as well as five to six professors.

There are two other university direct exchanges with Moscow State University. The Mid-West University Consortium for International Activities, representing eight Big Ten universities, exchanges two to three professors on each side annually. The University of Missouri exchanges one to two faculty members each year. An exchange between Rutgers and Kiev State University was negotiated in 1978, but the Ministry never gave its final approval.

A teacher exchange is conducted between the American Field Service and the USSR Ministry of Education. Begun by the American Friends Service Committee in 1961, this exchange has been run by the American Field Service since 1972. Six Soviet and six American teachers are exchanged for ten weeks each year, the longest period of time the Soviets have been willing to accept. The Americans teach English in special language secondary schools and teachers colleges in the Soviet Union. The Soviets teach Russian in high schools and colleges in the United States. This exchange, which has been privately run since its inception, was mentioned, for the first time, in the 1985 agreement.

Reciprocal exchanges are usually conducted on a cost-sharing basis under which the sending side pays international transport for the students it sends to the other country. This is also known by the Soviets as a "non-foreign currency exchange" since it permits them to spend only rubles on international exchanges—when the Soviets fly via Aeroflot, the Soviet airline. The American exchange partners spend dollars for the Soviets in the United States, but in some cases they also spend dollars for the Americans in the Soviet Union as well.

There are also several "one-way" exchanges under which American students study Russian in the Soviet Union, paying all costs in dollars, but no Russians study in the United States in exchange.

The largest of these is the Council on International Educational Exchange (CIEE) which has been sending American students to Leningrad State University for Russian-language study since 1966. CIEE sends about 210 students each year, mostly undergraduates, for a summer term, or one to two semesters during the academic year. The CIEE program is affiliated with thirty-four U.S. colleges and universities, but students from other institutions are also accepted. Since its inception, more than 4,000 Americans have studied Russian at Leningrad under the CIEE program.

Another 200 U.S. undergraduates study Russian each year at Moscow's Pushkin Russian Language Institute under a program administered by The American Council of Teachers of Russian (ACTR). Smaller one-semester programs at the Pushkin Institute are maintained by Ohio State–Purdue, with thirty-one persons each year, and Middlebury College, with thirty persons each year. The Ohio State–Purdue program is open to qualified students from other institutions.

The Soviets, for administrative reasons, would prefer to deal with a single agency for these Russian-language programs, and they have suggested, at times, merging the U.S. private programs into one organization, such as IREX, and mentioning it in the cultural agreement. U.S. officials have resisted this in the past, believing that the Soviets should learn to deal with the pluralism of U.S. education.

The Graduate Student / Young Faculty Exchange

After twenty-eight years of cultural exchange with the Soviet Union, it might be asked why there are so few students and scholars exchanged between two such large countries.

The answers lie mainly in the Soviet attitude toward exchanges with the West, and the difficulties which an open society has in attempting to cooperate with a closed society and a government which is paranoid in its suspicion of foreigners and archaic in its administration. The IREX Graduate Student exchange will serve to illustrate some of these difficulties, although they apply to many other exchanges as well.

Scholarly exchanges are regarded by the Soviets as an instrument of national policy, and exchange agreements are negotiated to achieve specific objectives. While IREX exchanges overall are mostly in the humanities and social sciences, some 80 to 90 percent of the Soviet Graduate Students under this particular IREX exchange are in science and technology.

The Soviet "Graduate Students" are mostly in their early or mid-thirties, have their *Kandidat* degree—which is somewhat less than our Ph.D.—and are conducting advanced research at Soviet science and technology research institutes. There is no Soviet open competition for these grants, but rather the Soviet researchers are selected and detailed to the United States on official duty status because their research topics are important to the Soviet Union. As a measure of how carefully the Soviet Graduate Students are selected, not one has defected in the United States since the exchange began in 1958. However, even in a planned society and police state, things go wrong.

In 1982, the Ministry was shaken by a scandal which disclosed that some Soviets had been buying their way into the exchange by bribing Ministry officials.

The Americans who go to the Soviet Union under this numerically reciprocal (one-for-one) exchange are mostly in their mid- or late twenties, and are either advanced graduate students who have completed all their course work and are doing research for their doctoral dissertations or they are young postdoctorals who are already teaching. They are selected in an open competition by a panel of scholars appointed by IREX, and almost all of them are in the humanities and social sciences.

Until the early 1970s, the Soviet Union would not accept Americans for research on contemporary—post-1917—topics, and for this reason very few American scholars in these fields would apply for the program. As a consequence, most of the American Graduate Students sent between 1958 and the early 1970s were in Russian history and literature—pre-1917—or Russian language studies. Since the early 1970s, there has been a more equitable representation of the social sciences and humanities among the Americans in the program.

Until the mid-1970s, American nominees for this exchange were given a routine security check by the State Department—the "name-check" procedure which asks the FBI, CIA and other intelligence agencies to report any information they may have on file. This procedure, which had been a requirement for all cultural exchange grantees supported by federal funds, was discontinued in 1975. Other than this, there has been no U.S. government attempt to influence the IREX selection process which is completely in the hands of the U.S. scholarly community.

The number of American and Soviet Graduate Students exchanged under the IUCTG and IREX programs has remained within a narrow range. The exchange began in 1958 with twenty persons on each side. Over the next three years there was a gradual increase to "at least 40"—the language used in the cultural agreement—but when U.S.-USSR relations cooled during the Vietnam War years, the quota was cut back to thirty in 1969, at Soviet request. With détente, another increase began, and the exchange reached its peak in 1975 when fifty-two persons were nominated and accepted on each side. Another decline began in 1980, after the Soviet invasion of Afghanistan and the lapse of the cultural agreement, and in the 1983–1984 academic year there were only twenty-four American Graduate Students in the Soviet Union. Twenty Soviets had arrived in the United States in September 1983, but they were recalled by Moscow after the Korean Airline disaster because Moscow feared for their safety after there were anti-

Soviet demonstrations in the United States. They returned to the United States in February 1984.

Thus, in 1984, the number of students exchanged was down to almost where it had been when the exchange began in 1958. In fact, a curve for the number of persons exchanged under this program would parallel, with a year or two time lag, a curve reflecting the state of U.S.-USSR relations.

The new cultural agreement signed at the Reagan-Gorbachev summit in 1985 provides again for the exchange of "at least" forty, and the number actually exchanged is expected to be close to this lower limit.

There are other reasons why this exchange has not grown, aside from the state of U.S.-USSR relations. First, it is a politically sensitive program for both governments—for the United States, because the Soviets do research in high technology, and for the Soviet Union, because the Americans do research in the fields of the social sciences and humanities which they consider sensitive. Second, high costs have been an inhibiting factor for the American side. Third, the pool of qualified American applicants has never been very large, and IREX has chosen not to lower its high standards of selection. Fourth, IREX has chosen to expand its exchange activities with the Soviets in other areas such as collaborative research in the social sciences and short-term exchanges of senior scholars.

In negotiating the cultural agreement, Soviet officials have always given a very high priority to the Graduate Student exchange and, except for the years when relations with the United States were strained, they have sought to increase the number of persons to be exchanged. Indeed, based on personal observation of Soviet tactics in the cultural negotiations for many years, it is clear that this exchange, in recent years, has been for the Soviets the most important part of the entire cultural agreement. The reason is the access to U.S. science and technology afforded by this exchange. As a consequence, the Graduate Student exchange has become embroiled in the complex issue of technology transfer.

Technology Transfer

All Soviets in the Graduate Student exchange are limited, in principle and with few exceptions, to fundamental research at U.S. universities and are denied access to industrial facilities and production technology. The exchange, nevertheless, has a potential for technology transfer, and procedures were established in the early years of the cultural agreement to control and limit the access of all Soviet exchange visitors to militarily sensitive technology, including, for example, computers, microelectronics, lasers, guidance and navigation, propulsion, acoustical sensors and radar.[3]

Soviet nominations for exchanges in science and technology, including those visa applicants who wish to attend scientific conferences, are reviewed by a U.S. government interagency group, the Committee on Exchanges (COMEX), a subcommittee of the Technology Transfer Intelligence Committee established in 1981 by CIA. Each Soviet nomination is screened by COMEX with regard to the nature of the proposed research and where it will be conducted, to determine if the research is permissible under the Export Administration Act of 1979, the U.S. law which regulates high technology exports.[4] After completing its review, COMEX gives an advisory opinion to the Department of State which decides whether the proposed research is acceptable, and whether a visa may be issued for it.

In the case of the IREX Graduate Student Exchange, COMEX, in its review, may determine that the subject of the proposed research is in a "militarily critical" technology. If State concurs, it informs IREX that a visa will not be issued for the proposed research, and IREX, in turn, informs the Ministry that it is unable to make arrangements for the requested research. COMEX may also recommend a modification of the research proposal to make it acceptable, or it may recommend that, while the proposed research poses a problem at one U.S. university, it may not at another. In such a case, the Soviet nominee may not be placed at his first-choice university. "His" is used here because the Soviets have not sent a woman under this exchange since IREX began to administer it in 1968. COMEX, furthermore, always requests that Soviet researchers be denied access to all research funded by the Department of Defense, unless access has been specifically approved by Defense.

To further limit access to technology by the Soviet Graduate Students, their travel in the United States in controlled. U.S. host universities are requested to inform IREX or the State Department of any travel planned by a Soviet student beyond twenty-five miles from the place of study. If the travel is for pleasure, no approval by State is required. But if the travel is for professional reasons, such as a visit to another university or attendance at a scientific meeting, advance approval by State is required.

Soviet authorities have never objected to this because their control of travel by American students in the Soviet Union is much more severe. Some 20 percent of the Soviet Union is closed to travel by all foreigners, including exchange students, and travel plans must be filed with the Soviet authorities in advance. Furthermore, travel requests by

American students to open areas, whether for scholarly or touristic reasons, are often denied.

In retaliation, the United States has closed about 20 percent of its territory to travel by Soviet citizens. These controls, however, do not apply to Soviet exchange visitors who are free to travel for pleasure to any part of the United States.

The United States has offered several times to abolish or reduce these travel restrictions on a mutual basis, but the Soviets have shown no interest.

The research proposals of the American graduate students may also present problems for the Soviets. The Americans, who will be the next generation of U.S. specialists on the Soviet Union, all speak Russian or another Soviet language, and their research proposals may be considered by the Soviets to be sensitive, particularly those dealing with contemporary Soviet society. Although the record of Soviet acceptance of U.S. social science research proposals has improved in recent years, there are many that still are not approved. Among the U.S. research proposals not accepted by the Soviets in the past two years are The Role of the Soviet Worker in the Management of Production, The Development of Soviet Thought on Revolutionary Change in the Third World, The Role of Local Soviets in Dealing with "Quality of Life" Issues, The Impact on Forecasts of World Market Conditions on the Planning and Implementation of Soviet Foreign Trade, Social and Economic Transformations Among Peoples of the Far North in the Soviet Period, and Neoprimitivism in Russian Painting and Poetry (1907–1914).

Due to this sensitivity to research proposals on both sides, the acceptance of nominees is subject to lengthy negotiations between IREX and the Ministry. Each side enters these negotiations with a list of nominees it can accept, those it must reject and others which are somewhere in between. Since the exchange is numerically reciprocal, there are tradeoffs until an agreed number is reached, usually less than the quota in the cultural agreement. In years when Soviet-American relations are good, these negotiations go smoothly, as in 1975 when all nominees were accepted on both sides, and fifty-two persons were exchanged. When relations are strained and the U.S. government has taken a harder position on technology transfer, the rejections may be high, as in 1983 when only twenty-four of the thirty-seven Soviet nominees were accepted. Thus, politics also determines how many Soviets are accepted or rejected.

The result of this complex procedure is that for each Soviet in high technology who is rejected by the U.S. side, an American is rejected by the Soviets, usually in a social science. This procedure, cumbersome as it is, has evolved over twenty-eight years and is accepted by both sides. For a limited number of American students, it assures access to research sources in the Soviet Union. Without the leverage on Soviet researchers exercised by IREX and the State Department, it is questionable how many Americans would be able to conduct scholarly research in the Soviet Union.

The high costs of the Graduate Student exchange, as compared with other exchanges, have also inhibited its growth. In 1986, it cost IREX $14,000 to maintain one Soviet Graduate Student in the United States, and $18,000 for one American in the Soviet Union, each for nine months, or a total cost of $32,000 for each pair of students exchanged.[5] The total U.S. cost each year for forty students on each side, the target quota in recent years, is $1,280,000. WIth costs increasing each year, funds to enlarge the program have not been available from either the U.S. government or the private sector. IREX, moreover, believes that the number forty is about right for this highly selective program.

It has been charged that the United States is bested in this exchange because it sends scholars in the "soft" social sciences whereas the Soviets send scientists and engineers in the "hard" sciences. There is indeed an asymmetry in the Graduate Student exchange. Some 80 to 90 percent of the Soviet participants are in the hard sciences, while American scientists very rarely participate. This is not because the Soviets will not accept them, but because American scientists find it more useful to make short visits to Soviet Union rather than spend a full semester at a Soviet university where the scientific gains may not be sufficiently attractive. Moreover, Soviet universities are mainly teaching, rather then research, institutions. The exchange between the National Academy of Sciences and the Soviet Academy better serves the needs of American scientists, but this exchange is limited to postdoctoral research and is not open to graduate students.

There is also a professional reason why it is difficult to recruit young American scientists for Soviet exchanges. Science is changing so fast today that a young scientist who leaves the United States for a year of study abroad may find, after returning home, that he is at a disadvantage in the competition for a good job. This is not true for young Soviet scientists, whose careers are greatly enhanced by a year abroad, particularly in the United States.

The hard vs. soft science argument overlooks the benefits of the research conducted by the American Graduate Students. Alumni of the IREX exchange are found at almost every American college or university with a Soviet studies program, helping another generation of Americans to better understand the Soviet Union. IREX alumni are also found increasingly in business, journalism, law and in virtually all branches of government where they bring not only a first-hand knowledge of the Soviet Union but also a "feel" for Soviet behavior that comes only with having lived there for a year.

The American students, who live on the Soviet economy and experience the daily life of Soviet citizens, return to the United States with a better understanding of the Soviet Union than American diplomats who lead a semi-isolated existence in Moscow imposed by the Soviet Union. The IREX alumni constitute a national asset in U.S. efforts to understand and deal with the Soviet Union.

As Alexander Dallin puts it, the Americans return from the Soviet Union with "an instinct that enables you to make confident judgments about what is plausible and what is ludicrous . . . and which reduce the likelihood of misperception or misinterpretation of Soviet behavior."[6]

It is ironic that, whereas the Americans enter the exchange with a relatively open mind on the Soviet Union, they return to the United States with a very sober and realistic view of Soviet society. The Jesuits used to say "Give us the boy and we shall have the man." The Soviets have these young Americans for a year, but they botch the opportunity to influence them favorably.

And what is the effect on the Soviets of an academic year in the United States? There is evidence that exposure to the United States through exchanges has an impact on Soviet perceptions of this country. Allen H. Kassof, IREX Executive Director, says:

. . . the miasmic visions of America on which several generations of Soviet citizens were raised during the Stalin years have not only given way to depictions that are at least grudging approximations of the reality, but in some cases are astonishingly accurate and insightful. And although only a very limited portion of this new fund of information is made directly available to the Soviet public, at the upper decision making levels there is now access to an elaborate, heavily funded and influential complex of research institutions that, in little more than a decade, has created a veritable army of Americanists.[7]

And Dallin adds:

. . . an inevitable by-product of the exchanges, [is] exposing Soviet scholars and students to more explicitly open and plural contexts, alternative approaches, techniques and values—to experiences that would make better and more objective scholars of them (and incidentally may also lead them to rethink some of their beliefs).[8]

As for the current whereabouts of Soviet alumni of the IREX exchange, no survey in the Soviet Union has been possible. However, most Soviet Americanists have been to the United States on IREX programs, and former IREX participants can be found throughout the Soviet scientific and scholarly communities as rectors (heads) of institutes, deans of faculty, chiefs of laboratories and professors. Two of the more prominent are Aleksander N. Yakovlev, currently a Party Secretary and head of the Propaganda Department, Central Committee of the Communist Party, and Boris Runov, a USSR Deputy Minister of Agriculture. Another IREX alumnus was Rem Khokhlov, the Rector (President) of Moscow State University, who died in a tragic mountain climbing accident in 1977.

The Corson Panel

IREX exchanges with the Soviet Union, as well as those of the National Academy of Sciences, came under scrutiny in 1982 when a prestigious Academy-appointed panel, chaired by Cornell University President Emeritus Dale R. Corson, was convened "to examine the effect on national security of technology transfer to adversary nations by means of open scientific communications, either through scientific literature or person-to-person communications. . . ." [9]

The focus of the Panel's study was on Soviet efforts to gain access to sensitive U.S. technology with defense applications, and whether controls on such activities would inhibit the free communication of scientific and technical information necessary to U.S. scientific achievements.

Admiral Bobby Inman, CIA Deputy Director, provided an authoritative statement to the Panel on the role of scientists and students in technology transfer to the Soviet Union. In testimony for a hearing on technology transfer conducted by the Senate Governmental Affairs Subcommittee on Investigations on May 11, 1982, and published by the Corson Panel, Inman estimated that 70 percent of Soviet bloc acquisitions of Western high technology is made through their intelligence services. Another 20 to 30 percent, he added, is made through legal purchases and Western published material. "Only a small percentage," Inman concluded, "comes from the direct technical exchanges conducted by scientists and students."[10]

The Corson Panel found that a substantial and serious technology transfer exists, but the evidence it reviewed failed to reveal specific evidence of damage to U.S. national security caused by information obtained from U.S. academic sources. The Panel concluded that, while academic exchanges have a potential for technology transfer, only a very small part of the lost technology can be attributed to the scientific tradition of open communication.

Regarding IREX exchanges with the Soviet Union, the Panel noted that most U.S. participants have found their visits to the Soviet Union to be satisfactory, and the program clearly advances U.S. graduate training in Soviet studies. As for the Soviet students, the Panel continued, a majority of their U.S. university hosts have reported their scientific performance to be at least satisfactory. On the issue of "soft" vs. "hard" research topics of the U.S. and Soviet students, the Panel noted the commonly perceived asymmetry of the exchange and its possible use for intelligence gathering purposes.

The Panel recommended that: (1) some fixed portion of the IREX program be reserved for technical and scientific fields in which the United States and the Soviet Union have rough parity; (2) review procedures on the receiving side be enhanced to ensure that only bona fide scholars are sent on exchanges; (3) all military sensitive areas be excluded from the exchanges by formal agreement; and (4) new or expanded procedures be developed to ensure that the program is mutually beneficial.[11]

These recommendations are not new. They have been considered previously on several occasions by State and IREX. But before examining them, there is another statement by Inman which should be noted because it is not evident that it was considered by the Corson Panel.

In the Senate hearing of May 11, 1982, on technology transfer, Senator Sam Nunn asked Inman about the IREX exchange:

We hear over and over again about how the Soviets send middle-aged scientists over as students, [while] we send students of Soviet history over in an exchange program. One is after technology, the other is after some form of legitimate literary or historical endeavor. There is nothing wrong with the latter but what is it you would like to see the scientific and intellectual community do in this regard and I stress voluntarily without government dictating. . . ?[12]

Inman replied:

. . . there are some exchanges that are clearly in our national interest. We are going to need in this decade out ahead scholars and students with language skills who can watch the actions of our adversaries and give us sound advice, whether they are working in the intelligence community as analysts, or whether they are working in the Foreign Service or other parts of the Government. And so we should be cautious as we go about assessing the value to this country of various area studies and language training as part of the exchange structure.[13]

The Corson Panel recommendation to set aside some portion of the IREX program for science and technology so as to remove the asymmetry in the exchange has been considered by State several times. In the early 1960s, State suggested to IUCTG that 50 percent of the U.S. students and no more than 50 percent of the Soviet students be scientists.[14] Similar proposals were made by State to IREX suggesting a quota for scientists among the U.S. nominations.

These proposals were rejected because both IUCTG and IREX believed that not enough qualified U.S. scientists could be found, since there is little incentive for them to apply. Moreover, the IREX Graduate Student exchange is with the USSR Ministry of Higher Education which represents Soviet universities—mainly teaching rather than research institutions. To conduct research in the Soviet Union, an American scientist would have to go on the National Academy of Science exchange with the Soviet Academy of Sciences which conducts much of the fundamental scientific research in the Soviet Union. Moreover, IREX—and IUCTG previously—believes that American students should be selected on the basis of their scholarly qualifications and research proposals rather than their academic disciplines. Efforts by State to correct the asymmetry were also seen by American scholars as government interference in scholarly exchanges.

The asymmetry issue has been discussed with the Soviets repeatedly. When U.S. officials, in December 1979, suggested that the Ministry take steps to end the asymmetry lest the large numbers of Soviet scientists and engineers cause difficulties for the Graduate Student Exchange, the issue was summarily dismissed by a Soviet Deputy Minister of Higher Education who pointed out that each side nominates candidates for the exchange in accordance with its own priorities and interests. (In this connection, about 75 percent of all graduate students in the Soviet Union are in science and engineering, whereas only 20 percent are in the United States.) In any event, the Soviet Union is unlikely to accept a quota for scientific fields in which the two countries have rough parity. Finally, a quota for scientific exchange would most likely destroy IREX's funding—always precarious—by such organizations as the National Endowment for the Humanities and those private foundations which have no interest in funding exchanges in science and technology with the Soviet Union.

"Review procedures to ensure that only bona fide scholars are sent on exchanges," the second recommendation of the Corson Panel, is presumed to apply to Soviet nominees, although the Soviets could be expected to apply any new procedures to U.S. students as well. IREX, in fact, does ensure, to the extent possible, that Soviet nominees are bona fide scientists. For each nominee, IREX requests a "data sheet" giving the nominee's academic background, places of study and employment, and titles of published research. The data provided by the Ministry is seldom complete, and IREX over the years has consistently pressed for more information which it needs to place the Soviet nominees in U.S. universities. There is little more that IREX or the U.S. government can do in this regard, given the closed nature of Soviet society, the limited U.S. access to data on Soviet scientists and scholars, and the fact that the Soviet nominees are usually in their early thirties and relatively unknown in the West. In any event, if a Soviet bona fide scientist has been co-opted by Soviet intelligence to gather information in the United States, he will be more effective at this assignment than a non-bona fide scientist.

Military sensitive areas, the Corson Panel recommended, should be excluded from exchanges by formal agreement. In principle, both sides could agree to this, but in this age of dual technology—applicable to both civilian and military use—who would decide what is military sensitive? If it can be charged that Soviet trucks produced at the Kama River plant with Western technology were used to transport the Red Army into Afghanistan, then diesel engines can be linked to tank production as well as to farm machinery, and computers to military as well as civilian use. Indeed, there is hardly a field of technology today that does not have both military and civilian application.

"Mutually beneficial," the final recommendation of the Corson Panel, has been a U.S. objective since exchanges began in 1958. Each side can argue that it is achieving its objectives and that the benefits are indeed mutual—the United States is training its future specialists on the Soviet Union, and the Soviet Union its future scientists and engineers. That these exchanges have continued for twenty-eight years after repeated assessments on both sides and even the suspension of the cultural agreement, would seem to argue that each side believes it is achieving its objectives and that continuation of the exchange is justified.

The broader, but unstated, issue in the Corson Panel recommendations is the extent to which scholarly exchanges with the Soviet Union should be regulated by the U.S. government as an instrument of policy. Many in the U.S. academic community have vigorously protested efforts by State to do just that, and both IUCTG and IREX have sought to protect their turf from government encroachment. The Graduate Student exchange, however, since its inception has been a part of the U.S.-USSR cultural agreement and, as a consequence, the U.S. government and IREX have been partners in a very complex relationship with the Soviet Union. This is unlikely to change.

The issues raised by the Corson Panel have never been resolved satisfactorily. Like many issues in Soviet-American relations there are no clear-cut solutions, only gradual accommodation by the two sides, intended to keep the dialogue going and to permit further accommodation at a later date.

Twenty-eight years of exchanges with the Soviet Union have shown that IREX or some other central agency is necessary for the U.S. scholarly community to deal effectively with the Soviet Union on reciprocal exchanges, to negotiate as coequal with the Ministry and the Soviet Academy, to ensure reciprocity for American students and scholars, to press for improved conditions for their work in the Soviet Union and to ensure that the exchanges are mutually beneficial.

If IREX were to become an agent of the U.S. government in its exchanges with the Soviet Union and Eastern Europe, it could no longer claim to represent academia. Under such conditions, many U.S. universities would be unwilling to cooperate with IREX and to waive their fees for Soviet students and scholars, thus requiring the government to pick up all costs of the exchange.

Some degree of U.S. government regulation of these exchanges is the price we have to pay for cooperation with the Soviet Union, since all dealings with the Soviets are essentially political. As Dallin puts it:

> I am compelled to say that I find the presence of political elements in the exchange on both sides inherent and inevitable. I do not see how it could be otherwise, given the nature of the Soviet system and of academic life. What is clear is that a delicate balance needs to be maintained, assuring on the one hand government involvement and commitment and on the other hand the independence of the program responsibly operated on behalf of the participating academic institutions. . . . It is equally important to avoid in the years ahead, either a withdrawal of government interest and support or any effort to "take over" what must be an agency by and for scholars.[15]

And 10,000 Students?

Eisenhower's 1958 proposal to exchange 10,000 undergraduates with the Soviet Union was never formally made. Eisenhower notes, however, that he went so far as to draft a letter to Chairman Bulganin offering to invite "several thousand" Soviet students to the United States, all expenses paid, leaving it up to the Soviets to decide whether to invite American students in exchange. His proposal was not made public, as he adds, because the State Department was negotiating a cultural agreement with the Soviets at the time and was having difficulty getting the Soviets to agree to exchange 100 students.[16]

Twenty-eight years later, another U.S. president, Ronald Reagan, was asking, "Why not suggest the exchange of thousands of undergraduates each year, and even younger students who would live with a host family and attend schools or summer camps?" and the prospects appear to be equally dim.[17]

The Soviets have shown some interest in exchanging small groups of secondary school students, accompanied by a Soviet teacher, and one such exchange is under active consideration. But it is most unlikely that they will agree to exchange individual students and to allow them to live with American families.

The prospects are also dim for an exchange of thousands of advanced graduate students for study and research, which is what the Soviets would want. An increase in this type of exchange would require major policy changes on each side. The Soviets would have to agree to send more students in the social sciences and humanities, ending the present asymmetry, and the United States would have to relax its export controls to permit more Soviet students to conduct high technology research. Both prospects are highly unlikely.

There is another category, however, undergraduates and beginning graduate students, for which there may be some possibilities. The Soviets, in the Gorbachev era, may be interested in this category, although not in the thousands suggested by two American presidents.

In 1983, only 30,000 college students in the United States were studying Russian, or about 3.6 percent of all students studying foreign languages, according to figures provided by the Modern Language Association.[18] Estimates for those studying Russian in 1986 are between 32,000 and 33,000 at the college level, and perhaps 9,000 at the secondary school level.

"Common sense dictates that a larger fraction of our businessmen, scientists, government employees and the general citizenry have a basic understanding of their Soviet counterparts," reported a commission established in 1983 by the American Association for the Advancement of Slavic Studies (AAASS) to study the language problem.[19]

Among the commission's recommendations was a proposal to expand the number of positions available in the Soviet Union for language study by American students. In 1983, 900 person-months were available to Americans each year, and the commission recommended that an increase of 50 percent be negotiated over the next five years. Scholarship money, it added, should be raised from government and private sources to help cover the high air fares to Moscow and the study costs in the Soviet Union.

The Soviet Union is willing to accept American undergraduates to study Russian if they pay in dollars. There is a limit, however, on how many can be accepted in Moscow and Leningrad, the best places to study because of the quality of Russian spoken there and the cultural attractions of those cities. Enrollments for foreign students are limited in both cities because of the needs of Soviet higher education and the commitments the Soviets have made to accept students from other countries. But while the Soviets may be willing to accept a few more American students to study Russian, they have little interest in sending their undergraduates abroad to study English or anything else, except on a very limited basis, in groups and under controlled conditions.

Cost is another inhibiting factor. In 1986, it cost about $4,400, including round-trip air fare, for an American to study one semester in the Soviet Union. Without scholarship aid, only affluent American students would be able to study in the Soviet Union.

Senator J. William Fulbright made a proposal in 1978 which would alleviate the funding problem. The author of the Fulbright Program, which used proceeds from the sale of surplus American property overseas at the end of World War II to fund student exchanges, made a similar proposal for the Soviet Union.

The United States and the Soviet Union signed an agreement in 1972 under which the Soviet Union agreed to pay $722,000,000 in full settlement of its World War II lend-lease debt. The Soviets made three payments, and the balance of $674,000,000 was to be paid in equal installments provided that the United States, as then expected, granted most-favored-nation status to imports from the Soviet Union. The Jackson-Vanik amendment to the Trade Reform Act of 1974, however, put an end to the Soviet lend-lease repayments.

Fulbright proposed that the 1972 lend-lease settlement be modified to provide that annual installments of the debt repayment shall "be devoted exclusively to the financing and promotion on a balanced basis of educational, cultural and related types of exchanges in order to promote understanding and cooperation between the peoples of each society."[20]

Half the funds, payable in rubles, would be used to pay the expenses of Americans in the Soviet Union, thus reducing the dollar burden to the Soviet treasury in its repayment of the lend-lease obligation. The other half of the Soviet payments would be made in dollars to the U.S. Treasury. They would be offset by an annual appropriation made by the Congress and equal to the Soviet payment, to be used for the dollar expenses incurred by the Soviets in the United States, and administered under the Mutual Educational and Cultural Exchange Act of 1961 (Fulbright-Hays).

Even after the Reagan-Gorbachev Geneva summit, it is not yet evident that the Soviet Union is ready to agree to a major expansion of student exchanges with the United States. Fulbright's idea, nevertheless, is sound and should be kept in mind for that day in the future when the two governments are ready to agree that greatly increased exchanges and much broader communication between the American and Soviet people are in their mutual interest.

Notes

1. Dwight D. Eisenhower, *Waging Peace, 1956–1961* (New York: Doubleday), p. 411.

2. *Open Doors: Report on International Educational Exchange, 1983/84* (New York: Institute of International Education, 1984), pp. 135–140.

3. *Soviet Acquisition of Western Technology*, a report of the Central Intelligence Agency, April 1982; reprinted in the *Congressional Record*, May 19, 1982, pp. S 5589–5594.

4. 50 U.S.C. 2401.

5. These figures, obtained from IREX, include IREX administrative overhead costs.

6. Alexander Dallin, "A Balance Sheet of Soviet-American Exchanges," in *A Balance Sheet for East-West Exchanges*, IREX Occasional Papers 1, no. 1 (New York: International Research and Exchanges Board, 1980), p. 65.

7. Allen H. Kassof, Statement for the Committee on Foreign Relations, U.S. Senate, in *Perspectives: Relations Between the United States and the Soviet Union* (Washington, D.C.: U.S. Government Printing Office, 1979), p. 436.

8. Dallin, "A Balance Sheet of Soviet-American Exchanges," p. 72.

9. *Scientific Communications and National Security*, 2 vols. (Washington, D.C.: National Academy Press, 1982).

10. *Scientific Communications* 1, p. 55.

11. Ibid., p. 74.

12. *Transfer of U.S. High Technology to the Soviet Union and Soviet Bloc Nations*, Hearings before the Senate Permanent Subcommittee on Investigations of the Committee on Government Affairs, U.S. Senate, May 1982 (Washington, D.C.: U.S. Government Printing Office, 1982), p. 248.

13. *Ibid.*, p. 248.

14. Robert F. Byrnes, *Soviet-American Academic Exchanges, 1958–1975* (Bloomington: Indiana University Press, 1976), p. 132.

15. Dallin, "A Balance Sheet of Soviet-American Exchanges," p. 75.

16. Eisenhower, *Waging Peace*, p. 411.

17. *Weekly Compilation of Presidential Documents* 21, no. 46 (Washington, D.C.: Office of the Federal Register, National Archives and Records Administration), p. 1401.

18. Richard I. Brod and Monica S. Devens, "Foreign Language Enrollments

in U.S. Institutions of Higher Education—Fall 1983," *ADFL Bulletin* 16, no. 2 (January 1985).

19. *Russian Language Study in the United States* (Stanford: American Association for the Advancement of Slavic Studies, 1983), p. 4.

20. J. William Fulbright, "Lend Lease Debts to Pay for Educational Exchanges," *Just for the Press* 1, no. 2 (January 1978).

5

Public Diplomacy and Other Exchanges

Introduction

A broad range of people-to-people exchanges with the Soviet Union has evolved over the past twenty-eight years, some sponsored by the U.S. government, others by private institutions with government funding and, in recent years, by the private sector with private funding. The common denominator in these efforts has been the face-to-face contact and dialogue they have facilitated between U.S. and Soviet citizens in a wide variety of professional fields.

These activities have been centrally controlled and directed on the Soviet side. On the American side, they began as a government effort in the early years of exchanges, but since the 1970s they have developed without government direction as more and more U.S. citizen groups have sought to establish direct contact with their counterparts in the Soviet Union.

The result has been a rapid growth of private-sector activity, particularly between 1980 and 1985 when government activity declined because of deteriorating political relations and the absence of a cultural agreement. Indeed, the drafters of NSC 5607—the 1956 U.S. policy paper for East-West exchanges—who foresaw only a minor role for the U.S. private sector, would be surprised to learn that it has far overtaken the government sector in the numbers of persons exchanged each year.[1]

Delegations and Seminars

Delegation exchanges have always been favored by the Soviets over individual exchanges. The delegation represents what the Russians call a *kollektiv* (collective), which is a Russian as well as a Soviet tradition, and is opposed to the Western emphasis on the individual. And in a delegation the Soviet authorities have more possibilities for representing the various elements in their society—the government, the party, the various ethnic groups, creative artists, women, workers and others.

Delegation exchanges were the rule for both sides in the early years of exchanges when the main objective was to learn about the other country. Delegations were exchanged in all fields covered by the cultural agreement, from science and technology to culture and education. They ranged in size from five to ten persons or more, and they usually visited for two weeks on study tours, being briefed on developments in their fields and getting an overview of the other country. On their return home, delegations were debriefed, reports were written and that was usually the end of the exchange. Follow-up was rare.

"Seminars"—what the British call a "round table"—became popular during the détente years when both sides were seeking ways to broaden communication and cooperation. With détente, there was also interest in moving to more substantive exchanges with continuity.

Under the seminar format, each side fields a delegation, and the two delegations meet for several days of in-depth discussion on a pre-arranged agenda of common interest, usually at an out-of-the-way retreat. This is followed, or preceded, by a tour of about a week. There is usually some follow-up activity such as another seminar, some joint activity and further exchanges.

The seminar is politically attractive to the Soviets because, with U.S. and Soviet delegations sitting at the same table, it implies equality between the two superpowers whose representatives meet as coequals. The seminar also gives the Soviets a platform for promoting Soviet positions to a captive audience of prominent Americans.

The first U.S.-USSR bilateral seminar was the Dartmouth Conference—named after the site of the first conference in this series—a meeting of prominent Americans and Soviets held in 1960 at Dartmouth College under the leadership of Norman Cousins, then editor of the *Saturday Review*.

The meeting resulted from a suggestion made to Cousins by President Eisenhower who thought that non-official meetings between citizens of the two countries could be useful in facilitating informal discussion of bilateral issues in a relaxed atmosphere and by exploring options which could not be taken up in official talks between the governments.

The Dartmouth conferences have been held at one- or two-year intervals, focusing on such topics as arms control, political and economic issues, trade, the Middle East and regional conflict management. The Soviet sponsor was originally, and still is, the Soviet Peace Committee, but in recent years a group from the research institutes of the Soviet Academy has done the advance planning and administrative work. On the U.S. side, an advisory group assembled by the Kettering Foundation has performed this function. The purpose of the Dartmouth Conference, Norman Cousins has said, was:

> ... to identify areas of opportunity for both countries to reduce tension. Obviously, we relayed the results of each conference to government. The conferences made it possible for both governments to try out certain ideas without penalty. . . . In this way a number of issues with respect to the test ban were aired very early. There is no doubt in my mind that the Dartmouth Conference had some part to play in the eventual treaty that came about.[2]

A series of similar meetings has been held by the United Nations Association of the United States (UNA) since 1969 under its Parallel Studies Program with the Soviet Union. UNA conferences have focused on such topics as the environment, peaceful nuclear explosions, conventional arms control, North-South economic issues and indebtedness in the Third World and Eastern Europe. The Soviet partner has been the USSR United Nations Association, but in recent years the research institutes of the Soviet Academy have played the lead role. The change in the Soviet partner in both the Dartmouth and UNA conferences, to the research institutes of the Soviet Academy, indicates the importance which the Soviet Union attaches to these meetings.

Soviet participants in both the Dartmouth and UNA conferences have come from the Academy research institutes, the government, the Party Central Committee staff, the press, and, more recently, the Army General Staff.

U.S. participants have included former cabinet members, directors of research institutions and foundations, businessmen, scholars and writers.

The U.S. participants are all private citizens, although many have formerly served at high levels in the government. They speak only for themselves, although they may float trial balloons on behalf of the government. The Soviets, by contrast, all represent and speak for their government.

Dartmouth and UNA have similar objectives, initiating discussion of topics not on the official negotiating agenda between the two governments, prodding the thinking of both governments on future issues, clarifying intentions, explaining sources of policy, exploring policy options and gaining access to those who have influence in foreign policy considerations. The value of these conferences has been to provide a channel for private dialogue between the two countries, particularly when relations are not good, and for indirect input to Soviet policy makers. The conferences have also been used by the Soviets to signal intentions and possible future moves in such areas as arms control, the Middle East, bilateral trade, and economic and scientific cooperation.

Harold H. Saunders, former Assistant Secretary of State for Near Eastern and South Asian Affairs and a participant in the Dartmouth Conferences, has written:

> The measurement for the success of nonofficial dialogue between nations should not be immediate impact on policy. Its success lies in its contributing a sensitive picture of the problems to be faced, and, as moments of impasse approach, alternative ways of approaching those problems. At those moments, it is the "ideas in the air" that, often as not, provide insight into new approaches. Those ideas can be developed, examined, and crystallized when citizens talk.[3]

Through these conferences, the Soviets keep current on a variety of views of U.S. political thought. The conferences also help the Soviets to better understand the policies of the current administration in Washington, and to assess the future course of U.S. policies—what the next administration might do. They also help Americans, both in and out of government, who do not deal directly with the Soviet Union, to better understand that country and its interests.

Critics of these conferences point out that, over the years, the same faces tend to show up, especially on the Soviet side, and an "old boy" network has developed. True, the Soviets often send the same people to meetings with Americans—those who have the confidence of the party, are experienced in debate with Americans and in presenting the Soviet viewpoint, and who speak English. Georgy Arbatov, Yuri Zhukov and other "old boys" are members of an elite group of Soviets who are cleared for foreign travel, very much enjoy this travel and regard it as one of the perks of having achieved status in the Soviet Union. Rank has its privilege in the Soviet Union too.

There is also a Russian reason why the Soviet "old boy" network persists in these and other bilateral meetings. In traditional Russian society—which still persists in the Soviet Union in many ways—older and more experienced people are believed to know best and should therefore represent their country abroad. And in a country where travel abroad is a privilege, not a right, the boss always has the first cut at any opportunity which arises.

There are also sound arguments in defense of the "old boy" network. A good working relationship with the Soviets takes time to develop. Americans who have dealt with Soviets over the years know that the Soviets feel more comfortable in the company of familiar faces, and they show confidence and trust only after several meetings. In the Soviet Union, when something needs to be done a citizen goes first, not to the person responsible, but to someone he knows who can perhaps help. Useful and productive discussions can be held between Americans and Soviets only after a good working relationship has been established. Thus, while efforts are made by Americans to bring new and younger people into these conferences, there are advantages to meeting repeatedly with some of the same people.

Patricia Derian commented on this aspect of U.S.-USSR conferences after attending one in Minneapolis in June 1983 sponsored by the Institute for Policy Studies. The former Assistant Secretary of State for Human Rights in the Carter administration wrote:

> The only way to comprehension is knowledge and experience. That won't come with meeting 10,000 Soviets or Americans once. It comes with meeting the same people over and over again, getting past opening statements and host/guest rituals to whatever else there is.[4]

Congress and Government Officials

Most high-level American political leaders have never visited the Soviet Union. Only 56 percent of U.S. Senators had visited there as of May 1986, and the number of House Members is even less, 36 percent, according to statistics kept current by the Federation of American Scientists.

For Soviet leaders the record is no better. Only twenty of 100 leading Soviet officials had visited the United States by 1981, according to a study by Radio Liberty.[5]

To correct this, Senator Robert Dole offered a sense of the Senate resolution in July 1983 that "travel by members of the Senate to the Soviet Union serves the interests of the United States and should be, and is hereby, encouraged."[6] A similar House resolution, offered by Reps. Paul Simon and Douglas Bereuter in February 1984, went one step further, endorsing travel by Soviet leaders to the United States as well as House Members to the Soviet Union.[7]

Sen. Mike Gravel in 1969 had introduced a bill which went even further, proposing to exchange 1,000 U.S. elected officials and an equal number of Soviet officials over a five-year period, including governors, mayors and state legislators, as well as congressmen.

Averell Harriman and George Kennan, both former U.S. ambassadors to the Soviet Union, testified in support of the Gravel bill. One of our basic difficulties with the Soviet Union, said Harriman, is the lack of understanding of the United States on the part of Soviet officials because very few of them have travelled in the West. And lack of knowledge of the Soviet Union on the part of U.S. officials, added Harriman, has contributed to our difficulties.[8]

The Soviets sought exchanges between their Supreme Soviet and the U.S. Congress in 1958 in the first cultural agreement, but the U.S. negotiators—and presumably the Congress—were hesitant, and it was agreed only to continue the discussions. It was not until 1962, under the third cultural agreement, that the two governments agreed to "render every assistance" to visiting officials of their national governments. In the same agreement there was also a new provision for exchanges between "municipal, local and regional governing bodies." [9]

In subsequent years, U.S. senators and congressmen visited the Soviet Union, but it was not until 1974 that the first official exchange took place when a Supreme Soviet delegation headed by Politburo member Boris N. Ponomarev visited the United States. A Senate delegation headed by Senators Hubert Humphrey and Hugh Scott made a return visit in 1975, and a House delegation headed by Speaker Carl Albert in 1978. Another parliamentary exchange followed before the Soviet invasion of Afghanistan forced a halt.

Congress has been reluctant, over the years, to have formal exchanges with the Soviet parliament. Domestic political considerations are one reason. Most congressmen don't win votes back home by going to the Soviet Union. There is also the time factor. Many Congressmen find the time to visit other countries. But they are reluctant to enter into formal exchanges because this obliges them to play host for the return visits to the United States. If the Congress can have formal exchanges with the Soviets, then why not with the parliaments of allies and other friendly countries? It is easy to imagine the time this would consume on the busy schedules of Senators and Representatives.

In addition, many Congressmen believe that formal exchanges with the Soviet Union equate the Congress to the Supreme Soviet and thereby give legitimacy to that body which purports to represent the Soviet people. When high officials of the two countries exchange visits, there is indeed an implied equivalency of position and stature, as well as legitimacy.

Chief Justice Warren Burger, for example, visited the Soviet Union in 1977 and invited his "counterpart," Chairman of the Soviet Supreme Court Lev N. Smirnov, to make a return visit to Washington. The position of the Soviet chief justice, however, is much lower in the Soviet system than in the U.S. system, and it is not the equivalent of the U.S. Chief Justice.

Smirnov's visit to the United States gave the Soviet judicial system much more respectability than it deserves, particularly in view of the role it has played in the suppression of Soviet human rights.

Smirnov, moreover, was the presiding judge in the notorious 1966 trial of Soviet writers Andrei D. Sinyavsky and Yuli M. Daniel, who were convicted of crimes against the state for having allowed their joint work to be published abroad without official permission. Sinyavsky was given the maximum sentence, seven years in a labor camp. Daniel was given five years. The protests in the Soviet Union against their trial marked the start of the Soviet dissident movement.

Prior to détente there were few visits to either country by cabinet-level officials. In the 1970s, however, the annual meetings of the U.S.-USSR joint commissions, established to monitor the eleven bilateral cooperative agreements, provided an opportunity for cabinet and subcabinet level officials to exchange visits. These too ended with the invasion of Afghanistan and the decisions of the Carter and Reagan administrations to discourage high-level contacts. These visits were resumed gradually in the mid-1980s as the Reagan administration sought to improve relations with the Soviet Union.

During the détente years there were also several exchanges of state governors and Soviet republic officials conducted by the National Governors Association, and exchanges of mayors by the U.S. Conference of Mayors. Both exchanges were suspended after 1979.

In conclusion, a start was made during the 1970s in exchanges of political and governmental leaders, but it was still far short of what the relationship between the two superpowers would call for, in view of the importance of the two countries to each other.

Young Political Leaders

Young American political leaders have shown no hesitation in engaging the Soviets in exchanges. Between 1971 and 1979, 165 Americans and 150 Soviets participated in meetings between young—forty and under—leaders on the rise in their countries' political systems.

The American Council of Young Political Leaders (ACYPL), representing young leaders of the Democratic and Republican parties, was the sponsor of these exchanges on the U.S. side. For the Soviets, it was the USSR Committee on Youth Organizations, the government agency responsible for the Komsomol, the Communist Party's youth division, and other Soviet youth organizations.

Most U.S. participants in these exchanges have been political leaders at the state and local levels where political careers in the United States usually start. They have included state legislators, city council members, staffers of public and party officials, as well as lawyers, journalists, businessmen and trade union officials. For most of the Americans, these seminars provided the opportunity for their first visit to the Soviet Union. But more important, the five days spent in debate with the Soviets provided a unique opportunity to understand issues in U.S.-USSR relations as seen from the Soviet as well as the American side, and the differences in culture, tradition and history which divide the two countries. The two sixteen-person delegations were divided among four subcommittees, facilitating rapport and discussion, often on a one-on-one basis, as well as socializing during the day and evening sessions.

Soviet participants have included Komsomol and party officials on the republic as well as national level, editors and journalists, scholars from the Academy institutes, scientists, engineers and workers—the professions from which the leaders of the Soviet Union have usually come. For most of the Soviets, the seminars have also provided their first and only opportunity to visit the United States.

What makes these seminars different from the Dartmouth and UNA seminars is the relative youth on both sides and the inclination to speak more directly, and at times quite vociferously, without the diplomatic niceties and restraint that characterize the "older" seminars. Soviets appreciate and respect straight talk from their adversaries. They got it from the young American political leaders, and they responded in kind.

These exchanges were funded in their first year by the Ford Foundation, and in subsequent years by the State Department, until 1978 when USIA took over. They were interrupted by the Carter administration's suspension of cultural exchanges following the Soviet invasion of Afghanistan, and were resumed in December 1984. In 1986, two seminars were scheduled to be held in each country, funded as in the past by USIA.

Many U.S. participants in these seminars have already reached positions of influence where their Soviet experience has been useful. These include three Members of Congress, a State Governor, Lieutenant Governor, State Attorney General, Chairman of the Republican National Committee, Vice-Chairman of the Democratic National

Committee, Chairman of the White House Domestic Policy Council, Special Assistant to the President, State Department Spokesman, National Security Council staffer, university president, college president, syndicated columnist, editor of a newsletter and corporation president.

On the Soviet side it is too early to see upward movement, given the priority that age has had within the Soviet leadership. But because so many Komsomol leaders in the past have gone on to higher positions in the party and government, it can be assumed that many participants in these seminars will also, particularly in the Gorbachev era which is bringing a new generation of Soviet leaders to power.

One evidence of effectiveness of these seminars has been the change in the Soviet delegations' understanding of the United States and U.S.-USSR bilateral issues. Soviet delegates to the first seminar in 1971 were almost totally ignorant about the United States. With their distorted view of history they had limited ability to discuss substantive issues in Soviet-American relations and, as a consequence, they were no match for the U.S. delegation. Since that time, the Soviets have fielded better delegations and made certain that they were better informed about the realities of the United States and U.S.-USSR relations.

The U.S. participants' views of the Soviet Union have also been changed by these seminars. As one American delegate reported after a seminar in the Soviet Union, the conservatives in the U.S. delegation found that they had more in common with the Soviets than they had anticipated, while the liberals discovered that they had less.

More Public Diplomacy

Several new policy issue seminars have been held in recent years sponsored by such diverse U.S. groups as the Institute for Policy Studies of Washington, D.C., the Foreign Policy Research Institute of Philadelphia and the Esalen Institute of San Francisco. More recently, there have been larger meetings involving U.S. and Soviet citizens sponsored by the Chautauqua Institute, as well as television linkups by satellite between the two countries. Other U.S. sponsors of seminars with the Soviets include women's organizations, youth groups, religious groups and peace activists.

These meetings with the Soviets on a broad range of issues reflect a public concern that the U.S. government has not been doing enough to communicate with the Soviet Union, and that dialogue with the Soviets should be conducted, not only through official channels, but should be broadened through public diplomacy to include private citizens. In this regard, it is ironic that the Reagan administration, by continuing the Carter administration's suspension of cultural exchanges between 1980 and 1985, left the field wide open to citizen groups, many of which are opposed to its policies on the Soviet Union.

U.S. public dialogue with the Soviet Union should be broadened and the participation of all groups should be welcomed. U.S. citizen groups, however, should understand with whom they are meeting. The Soviets, in their meetings with U.S. citizen groups, staff their delegations with seasoned and skilled propagandists who are veterans of international exchanges. They speak, not for themselves, but for the Soviet government. The Americans who debate with these experienced polemicists are often not in the same league.

The Americans in these meetings, by contrast, speak only for themselves, but they bear a responsibility in also representing the United States. This does not mean to imply that they should necessarily defend the administration's policies. Rather, they should try to help the Soviets to understand the U.S. political process, the wide range of opinion on public issues, and how these views are ultimately presented, through elections, to the Congress and the White House. The Americans, above all, should avoid being used by the Soviets for political purposes. Public diplomacy can do some good in U.S.-USSR relations, but it can also do much harm in misrepresenting the United States to the Soviets. It's bad enough to have the United States attacked from one side of the table, without it being attacked from the other side as well.

Llewellyn Thompson, one of our most astute observers of the Soviet Union, commented on the hazards of dealing with the Soviet Union. In his final meeting with American correspondents in Moscow, just prior to leaving after completing his second assignment there as American Ambassador, Thompson was asked what he regarded as his greatest accomplishment. "That I didn't make things any worse," he replied.

The International Visitor Program

There are many other exchanges which don't make the headines. One is the International Visitor Program which brings Soviet professionals to the United States for visits up to thirty days in length. Originally conducted and funded by the State Department, this program since 1978 has been the responsibility of USIA. The Soviets, in exchange, have permitted the U.S. Embassy in Moscow to bring in American speakers on a broad range of subjects, under USIA's American Participant Program, to meet with Soviet counterparts in their fields of expertise.

Trips abroad for Soviet citizens, it has been charged, are payoffs for party loyalty and ideological orthodoxy. This is certainly true in many cases, and the practice is not unknown in other countries, including our own. Critics of cultural exchanges also charge that many of the Soviets who come to the United States are party officials and even members of the KGB. Statistics are not kept on how many Soviet visitors to the United States under the cultural agreement are party officials, but if the U.S. objective is to reach the leadership of the Soviet Union, this would be a good place to start.

Among the Soviets who have come to the United States under the International Visitor Program are such internationally respected persons as composers Dmitri Shostakovich, Dmitri Kabalevsky and Rodion Shchedrin; poets Andrei Voznesensky and Yevgeny Yevtushenko; theater directors Oleg Yefremov, Anatoly Efros and Galina Volchek; writers Valentin Katayev, Yuri Trifonov, Chengiz Aitmatov, Vitaly Korotich and Vladimir Soloukhin; and playwright Mikhail Roshchin. To get persons of this caliber, the United States has had to accept some of the others as well.

Notes

1. The text of NSC 5607 is appended as Appendix A.

2. Maureen R. Berman and Joseph E. Johnson, *Unofficial Diplomats* (New York: Columbia University Press, 1977), p. 6.

3. Harold H. Saunders, "When Citizens Talk: A Look at Unofficial Dialogue Between Nations," *The Kettering Review*, Summer 1984.

4. *Washington Post*, June 9, 1983, p. A19.

5. *A Biographic Directory of 100 Leading Soviet Officials, Radio Liberty Research Bulletin* (Munich, 1981).

6. Senate Resolution 182, July 25, 1983.

7. House Resolution 412, February 10, 1984.

8. *Exchanges of U.S.-U.S.S.R. Officials.* Hearing Before the Committee on Foreign Relations, United States Senate, 91st Cong. 2d sess., on S. 3127, To Provide for the Exchange of Government Officials Between the United States and the Union of Soviet Socialist Republics. Washington, D.C.: U.S. Government Printing Office, 1970, pp. 24–42.

9. *United States Treaties and Other International Agreements*, 5112, vol. 13, pt. 2, 1962, pp. 1496–1562.

6

Information

Introduction

Information exchanges—motion pictures, radio and television, and books and publications—are the most ideological exchanges for the Soviet Union because they threaten its monopoly on information. These exchanges, therefore, proved to be the most difficult for the United States to carry out under the cultural agreement.

The Soviets insist on retaining full control over what is reported in their media, about the Soviet Union as well as the outside world. And until Soviet censorship of outgoing press despatches by foreign correspondents was lifted in 1961, all information that was exported and imported had to be ideologically acceptable. This was to cause great difficulties for the United States—both the government and the private sector—in its attempts to conduct media exchanges with the Soviet Union and to bridge the barriers to a freer flow of information.

The commercial factor in these exchanges presented an added difficulty. The media of both countries seek to earn a profit from the sale of their products abroad, and this was one of the incentives for proposals for exchanges of motion pictures, books and publications, and radio and television programs through commercial channels.

Hopes were high when the first cultural agreement was signed, but the initial optimism of U.S. media representatives soon gave way to the harsh realities of attempting to do business with the Soviets in an ideologically sensitive area.

Motion Pictures

Both countries have very large film industries and huge domestic audiences, and the motion picture industries of the two countries had high expectations in 1958 when the first cultural agreement was signed. The section of the agreement dealing with motion pictures was the longest of the entire agreement, reflecting the role it was expected to play in cultural exchanges. But the initial optimism and subsequent effort did not pay off, and by 1986 only a handful of films were being sold between the two countries each year.

The U.S. government also saw the cultural agreement as a vehicle for showing documentary films in the Soviet Union, and USIA was designated as the lead agency on the U.S. side for exchanging these films with the Soviets. Here too, after several years, the results were disappointing.

The first cultural agreement provided for a broad range of activities including the sale of films, film premieres in the two countries, exchanges of documentary films and film delegations, joint productions, film weeks and the production of films by one country in the other. To resolve problems which might arise in carrying out these provisions of the agreement, a standing committee was formed consisting of two members from each country who met twice yearly in Moscow and Washington.

The role of the U.S. government in these exchanges was unusual. Under the terms of the cultural agreement, Sovexportfilm, the state film monopoly, was to "enter into contract with representatives of the motion picture industry in the United States, to be approved by the Department of State . . . for the purpose of the sale and purchase of films. . . ."[1] And before a U.S. film was offered to the Soviets under the agreement, it became practice to have it screened by the State Department to determine its suitability for sale. This practice was discontinued only in the early 1970s. The cultural agreement, moreover, applied only to members of the Motion Picture Association of America (MPAA), the major producers, and did not cover the independent studios which were free to deal with the Soviets outside the agreement. Here was the first indication to the Soviets that they could deal with elements of the U.S. film industry without an agreement.

The potentially huge market for films in the two countries was real, and a good start was made when the first contract, negotiated by MPAA president Eric Johnston, was signed in 1958 for ten U.S. and seven Soviet films.

Soviet films initially were popular with the U.S. public, and several films were also critical successes, including "My Name is Ivan," "Ballad of a Soldier" and "The Cranes are Flying." The initial interest, however, soon wore off. American audiences don't like subtitled or dubbed films, and foreign films generally do not do well in the United States. And the Soviet films, with few exceptions, were not of interest to the U.S. mass audience. Americans found them dull, didactic and ideological.

American films, by contrast, were box office successes in the Soviet Union. The Soviets, however, tended to purchase films which were critical of American society and were therefore ideologically acceptable—and this has not changed in the 1980s.

There were also financial problems. The Soviets refused to pay a fixed fee and a percentage of box office sales for films they purchased, as is customary in other countries. They agreed, instead, to pay only a fixed fee in hard currency which was negotiated for each film, but at less than the normal price. Each side accused the other of demanding exorbitant prices for its films.

These basic difficulties could not be overcome by the standing committee and it was dissolved after 1965.

The exchange of documentary films fared no better. The Soviets were unwilling to show most of the films offered by USIA, and they soon learned that they could place their own films in the United States without going through the cultural agreement.

The Moscow International Film Festival, in its early years, had official U.S. entries and high-level MPAA delegations. But this too ended as the sale of films dwindled. In recent years only individual American studios have chosen to participate in the festival, and there have been no official U.S. film entries. Moreover, U.S. producers are reluctant to send films to Moscow for screening, either for the festival or for purchase, because the Soviets are known to make copies and to show them without paying a fee.

Soviet films, in recent years, have been doing better in the United States, showing mostly on the art theater circuit. "Moscow Does Not Believe in Tears" won an Oscar in 1980 as the best foreign film, and several other Soviet films have won prizes at U.S. film festivals. But the big commercial success that the Soviet Union had hoped for has been elusive.

Many of the U.S. films purchased by the Soviets are actually European films produced in Europe by U.S. companies. But, over the years, the five or so American films purchased annually by the Soviets have included such memorables as "Marty," "Roman Holiday," "All About Eve," "Twelve Angry Men," "Inherit the Wind," "Some Like It Hot," "To Kill a Mockingbird," "Zorba," "My Fair Lady," "Romeo and Juliet," "Around the World in 80 Days," "Lust for Life," "West Side Story," "Kramer vs. Kramer," and "Tootsie." Not a bad representation for U.S. cinema.

Radio and Television

Radio and television broadcast exchanges are another activity which was conducted, at the start, almost entirely between the two governments under the cultural agreement, but which subsequently became a completely private sector activity.

Broadcast exchanges were high on the U.S. request list when negotiations for the cultural agreement began in 1957, reflecting the U.S. desire to break through the information barrier to the Soviet audience. It also reflected the special interests of USIA whose mission was to tell America's story to the world—to explain and interpret the objectives and policies of the U.S. government abroad, particularly through American life and culture.

The 1958 cultural agreement provided for the exchange of radio and television broadcasts in all fields covered by the agreement as well as "international political problems." For broadcasts on the latter subject the agreement noted that they should "further the strengthening of friendly relations," and texts should be agreed to in advance. The 1959 agreement added a further qualifier to enable either party to reject a broadcast if it believed it did not contribute to improved relations. Programs were to be exchanged through Soviet Radio and Television and USIA.

Soviet programs, at the start, were not difficult to place on U.S. radio and TV stations, particularly if they were on music, theater, and other cultural subjects. The placement record, in the early years, was rather good.

Placement of U.S. broadcasts in the Soviet Union was much more difficult, and the record there was poor, even with purely cultural programs.

Both sides soon learned that there were limits to what they could expect the other side to place for them. Soviet films such as "Jews in the USSR" and "The Baltic Republics" had to be returned by the United States as being "inappropriate" for showing under the agreement. More difficult, if not impossible, to place were such films as "How Labor Disputes are Settled in Soviet Enterprises."

Among the U.S. television programs not broadcast by the Soviets were a biography of President Lyndon B. Johnson and an interview with Martin Luther King.

Moscow, after a few years of attempting to place its programs through U.S. government channels, began to deal directly with the U.S. networks and individual stations. By the end of 1965 the placement of programs under the agreement was down to zero, and the exchange of broadcasts was deleted from the agreement in 1968. All that remained was a general commitment to promote exchanges in radio and television, and to exchange delegations and individuals in these fields.

The Soviets had learned that they could place their own programs on U.S. networks without having to accept American programs in exchange. They had also learned that the U.S. networks were interested in producing their own TV films in the Soviet Union and were willing to pay the costs in hard currency.

In the 1970s and the heyday of détente, some of the U.S. networks signed cooperative agreements with the USSR State Committee for Radio and Television to exchange broadcasts and to assist each other in television productions. What they had in mind, perhaps, was the possibility of snaring the lucrative contract for coverage of the 1980 Moscow Olympics, which eventually went to NBC. This was the first major cooperative effort between U.S. and Soviet television, and it demonstrated that cooperation is indeed possible, if the interests are mutual and the price is right.

Books and Publications

The Soviet Union and the United States are the world's largest book publishers. One might expect, therefore, that there would be a brisk trade in books and publications between the two countries. Not so, unfortunately.[2]

Trade in science and technology books and publications is active in both directions. The science communities in both countries are approximately equal in size, and much of what is published in one country is of interest to scientists of the other. Scores of Soviet science journals are published in the U.S. in English translation, under license, as are many U.S. science journals in the Soviet Union. There is also an active trade in rights to books in science and technology which are published in translation in each country. Editions of two to three thousand copies are the norm.

In the mass market book trade, however, sales are limited by differences in style, reader interest and ideology. Soviet authors, with few exceptions, simply do not sell well in the United States. By contrast, there is an enormous interest in American literature in the Soviet Union. The Soviets are avid book readers, but American authors are published in small editions which do not satisfy public demand, and only those works are published which are ideologically acceptable. For example, two U.S. Nobel laureates, Saul Bellow and Isaac Bashevis Singer, are not published in the Soviet Union because they are Jewish.

The book trade between the two countries was also handicapped for many years by Soviet refusal to recognize copyrights. Tsarist Russia had never acceded to an international copyright convention, and the Soviet Union did so in 1973 only with hesitation and after long deliberation. Two questions were crucial in this decision—would it be financially advantageous to recognize international copyrights, and would the Soviet Union be able to control publication abroad by its dissident authors. Apparently, the Soviet Union believed that the advantages in signing the copyright convention outweighed the disadvantages.

The cultural agreement provides a yardstick for measuring the slow and cautious movement of the Soviet Union in book and publication exchanges with the West and toward recognizing international copyrights. The first cultural agreement in 1958, reflecting Soviet interests, provided only for exchanges of publications in science and technology, medical journals, textbooks and pedagogical literature. Exchanges between libraries of the two countries were added in 1959, and magazine and newspaper exchanges in 1962. The 1962 agreement, moreover, provided that exchanges could also take place through commercial channels, and it mentioned, for the first time, exchanges of journalists, editors and publishers.

The first U.S. publishers delegation to the Soviet Union, in 1962, sought unsuccessfully to persuade the Soviets to accede to a copyright convention. That visit, however, began a dialogue between the two publishing industries which eventually helped persuade the Soviets to accede to the Universal Copyright Convention in 1973.

Soviet accession to the convention raised new possibilities for the book trade. Exploratory talks with Soviet publishers were held in Moscow in 1975 by Townsend Hoopes, President of the Association of American Publishers. As a result, twelve American publishers went to Moscow in 1976 for a week of discussions with Soviet publishers. Their main purpose, as in so many other initial contacts between Americans and Soviets, was to help each side to understand the other's practices so that they could learn to do business with each other.[3] At a second meeting one year later, fourteen Soviet publishers continued the discussions in New York.[4]

With each side now having a better understanding of the other, the ground was prepared for an increase in the sale of authors' rights and in joint publishing endeavors.

The new dialogue between publishers was marred, however, by the issue of whether Soviet authors could deal directly with U.S. publishers, and it was never satisfactorily resolved. As one American publisher puts it, the human rights minuet was danced ritually at almost every meeting between U.S. and Soviet publishers.[5]

The Moscow International Book Fair was one forum where publishers of the two countries could meet and do business, but it too was marred, from the start, by censorship of books exhibited at the fair and by violations of human rights in the Soviet Union. Although the American book exhibits were very popular with the Moscow public, book sales at the fair did not meet American expectations. U.S. publisher participation in the fairs decreased over the years as much of the initial interest declined and many publishers found that they could do business with the Soviets without the expense and hassle of participating in the fairs.

The Soviets publish more American authors than the United States publishes Soviet authors, and they cite copious statistics to prove this. The statistics can be misleading, however.

The Soviet Union is a multilingual society, and American authors are published in several language editions, each of which the Soviets tally as one American title. Moreover, many of the American books published by the Soviets are classics by such authors as Mark Twain and Jack London, and are in the public domain.

By contrast, fewer Soviet authors are published in the United States, and in smaller editions. The United States, similarly, publishes many editions of the classic Russian nineteenth century authors.

The Soviet Union is pleased by the publication abroad of classic Russian authors, but what it wants most is the publication of contemporary Soviet authors, in exchange for the contemporary American authors which it publishes. This theme is raised at every bilateral meeting on publishing and the book trade, where it is supported by Soviet statistics. The motive is to earn dollars and to support the dissemination of Soviet culture abroad.

That the Soviet statistics are misleading has been shown in a study prepared by Maurice Friedberg, Professor of Slavic Languages at the University of Illinois.[6]

The differences in books published in the two countries, says Friedberg, are explained by the different ways the two publishing industries function. While the Soviets publish larger editions of American authors, they are immediately sold out and cannot be purchased anywhere in the Soviet Union. In the United States, smaller editions of Soviet authors are published, but they remain in print and can be ordered from any U.S. book store. Furthermore, Soviet and Russian literature is widely available in U.S. public and university libraries, whereas this is not true for American literature in the Soviet

Union. Soviet and Russian literature is widely taught in U.S. universities, while this is not true for American literature in the Soviet Union.

The demand for Soviet books in the United States is satisfied, adds Friedberg, a demand not very large to begin with, because of differences in style and reader interest. In the Soviet Union, however, the huge demand for American books is not met. Also, any American can order books in Russian or other Soviet languages through a number of book stores in the United States which specialize in Soviet publications, but Soviet citizens cannot do the same for American books in English.

The United States, Friedberg concludes, has become a large repository for Russian and Soviet literature which is not published in the Soviet Union, as well as a haven for Soviet emigre authors. The works of many great Russian and Soviet writers, banned in the Soviet Union because they are ideologically unacceptable, are freely available in the United States in the original as well as in English translation.

Soviet publishers believe there are political reasons behind the poor sales of Soviet books in the United States, although American publishers have told them time and again, "If we can sell it, we'll publish it."

The brisk trade in science and technology publications bears this out. More than 100 Soviet scientific and medical journals are published in the United States in English translation each year. And more than thirty U.S. science and technology periodicals are published by the Soviets in Russian.

Scientific American, for example, the prestigious monthly, has been published in the Soviet Union in a Russian-language edition since 1983, with royalties paid in dollars. In 1986, 20,000 copies were being sold by subscription, and 5,000 by newsstand sales.

Human rights cannot be blamed for the failure of the U.S.-USSR book trade to develop. Some U.S. publishers believe the Soviets could sell far more books in the U.S. market if they could only better organize themselves to do so. When the Soviets publish books that will sell in the U.S. mass market and promote those books aggressively, they will be purchased by U.S. publishers and booksellers.`

Library Exchanges

Exchanges between U.S. and Soviet libraries have a long history, and they work surprisingly well.

The Library of Congress exchange with Soviet libraries began in the 1920s, was interrupted by World War II and was resumed in 1946.

Currently, the Library of Congress has seventy-four active exchange partners in the Soviet Union, including an official exchange of government documents, scientific periodicals and newspapers with Moscow's Lenin State Library.

University library exchanges work equally well. Most major U.S. university libraries have had active book and publication exchanges with Soviet libraries for many years. The University of Illinois, for example, which has the third largest Slavic collection in the United States, currently has active exchange relationships with some 100 libraries in the Soviet Union and more than 150 in Eastern Europe. Each side sends its own publications and also attempts to fill requests from the other side for specific titles. Fields covered by these exchanges include the humanities and social sciences, as well as science and technology. The Illinois Slavic Reference Service, through its exchanges with Soviet and East European libraries, processes more than 100 requests a month from scholars all over the world seeking Soviet and East European publications.

Amerika and *Soviet Life*

Monthly illustrated magazines are exchanged by the two governments under the cultural agreement, *America Illustrated—Amerika* in Russian—and *Soviet Life* in English. Both are glossy, large format publications, copiously illustrated with photographs and art work, and designed to show life in one country to the people of the other in the best possible light.

This exchange began during World War II, was suspended in 1952 and was revived in 1956 under an agreement between USIA and Soyuzpechat, a Soviet state publication agency. Like other U.S.-USSR information exchanges, this one has been beset with problems from the start, and neither magazine has fully realized its potential. This exchange predates the cultural agreement and it was continued during the suspension of the agreement between 1980 and 1985.

Amerika is the only U.S. government publication officially available to the Soviet public. Published by USIA, it is distributed in the Soviet Union through subscriptions and newsstand sales, as is its counterpart in the United States, *Soviet Life*, published by the Novosti Press Agency.

Under the terms of the cultural agreement, each side may distribute 60,000 copies of its magazine monthly, with an additional 2,000 for distribution by its embassy. This is where the similarities end.

The only impediment to the sale of *Soviet Life* in the United States is its reader appeal, which is not very great. Although it has improved in recent years—thanks largely to the example set by *Amerika*—*Soviet Life* is still heavy with "freight," the political articles which promote the policies and ideology of the Soviet Union. The magazine's writing and editing are old fashioned, even quaint, by U.S. standards. This would normally be of no concern to Americans except that *Soviet Life* does not sell well in the United States and, as a consequence, the sale of *Amerika* in the Soviet Union has been limited by the Soviet authorities.

Each month about 8,000 copies of *Amerika* are returned to the U.S. Embassy in Moscow as "unsold." The magazine, however, is extremely popular with the Soviet public. U.S. diplomats check newsstands in Moscow and Leningrad each month and confirm that the magazine is indeed on public sale and sells briskly. Copies available to the public, however, are very limited. Queues form up for the few copies on sale which go very fast, and many copies are held under the counter for preferred customers. When the Voice of America broadcasts in Russian that unsold copies of *Amerika* will be distributed at a designated hour to visitors at a USIA exhibition, Soviet citizens queue up for several city blocks at the announced hour.

Random checks around the Soviet Union by embassy officers have disclosed that the magazine is well known. There is a black market for back issues which get more than the newsstand price of fifty kopeks. USIA estimates that it could easily sell 500,000 copies each month, yet it is limited to the 60,000 specified in the agreement because *Soviet Life* sales in the United States do not meet that target,. Exact figures are not available, but it is estimated that *Soviet Life* sells perhaps only half its 60,000 copies.

USIA has offered practical advice to the Soviets on how to increase the distribution of *Soviet Life*. Changes in format and style have been suggested. The Soviets have been put in touch with U.S. firms which promote sales of publications, for a fee of course. Although these promotional efforts are guaranteed to produce results, the Soviets have been reluctant to spend in order to earn.

Conclusion

Information exchanges are yet another example of how the U.S. government initially tried to conduct exchanges with the Soviet Union in a field which is almost entirely in the hands of the private sector. That the private sector has not done much better than the government is mainly due to Soviet obsession with maintaining strict control over information which is disseminated within its territory, and making certain that it is ideologically acceptable. This is not likely to change much in the Gorbachev era.

Notes

1. *United States Treaties and Other International Agreements* 3975, vol. 9, 1958, p. 16.

2. For a report on Soviet publishing, see Herbert R. Lottman, "The Soviet Way of Publishing," *Publishers Weekly*, September 18, 1978, pp. 101–137.

3. For a report of this meeting, see Bradford Wiley and Townsend Hoopes, "A Publishing Summit in Moscow," *Publishers Weekly*, November 8, 1976, pp. 22–24.

4. See "14 Soviet Publishers Have 'Useful' Visit in U.S.," *Publishers Weekly*, November 28, 1977, pp. 11–13.

5. Martin P. Levin, "Soviet International Copyright: Dream or Nightmare?" *Journal of the Copyright Society of the U.S.A.* 31, no. 2 (December 1983), pp. 127–162.

6. Maurice Friedberg, *A Helsinki Record: The Availability of Soviet Russian Literature in the United States* (New York: U.S. Helsinki Watch, 1980).

7

Science and Technology

A Review (1958–1986)

Science and technology (S & T) are not usually regarded as cultural, but some S & T exchanges have been a part of the cultural agreement since its inception. Moreover, they involve people as well as laboratories, and the exchange of people is what cultural exchanges are all about. And because they often result in technology transfer, S & T exchanges have attracted attention from some critics of Soviet-American exchanges who charge that the Soviets are "stealing us blind."

The United States and the Soviet Union have the world's largest scientific communities, and it is understandable that there should be high interest in science exchanges on both sides. Scientists the world over consider themselves to be part of an international scientific community, and they want to stay in touch in order to keep current on what is being done in their fields.

S & T exchanges between the two countries in the postwar period began in 1958 under the first cultural agreement which included exchanges of delegations in industry, agriculture and medicine. As study tours of three to four weeks duration, they were intended to give each side an overview of what the other was doing in a particular field of science or technology.

Exchanges in the fundamental sciences began in 1959 with an agreement between the U.S. National Academy of Sciences and the Soviet Academy of Sciences. This agreement, which was annexed to the cultural agreement in 1962, provided for short-term exchanges of scientists for delivering lectures, conducting seminars and familiarization with scientific research, and long-term exchanges for scientific research and advanced study.

A memorandum of cooperation between the U.S. Atomic Energy Commission and the USSR State Committee for the Peaceful Uses of Atomic Energy was annexed to the cultural agreement in 1968. This provided for short-term exchanges of delegations and specialists, long-term exchanges of specialists for research, exchanges of information and joint conferences.

At the Nixon-Brezhnev summit meetings of 1972, 1973 and 1974, the S & T exchanges were spun off from the cultural agreement when eleven bilateral agreements were signed for cooperation in various fields of science and technology of common interest to the two countries.

These cooperative agreements were in Science and Technology, Environmental Protection, Medical Science and Public Health, Space, Agriculture, World Ocean Studies, Transportation, Atomic Energy, Artificial Heart Research and Development, Energy, and Housing and Other Construction.

For each agreement, a "lead agency" was designated by each government and a joint committee established, cochaired by cabinet or subcabinet level officials of the two countries, which met annually to review ongoing work under the agreement and to make plans for future activities. Altogether, some 240 working groups of U.S. and Soviet scientists were established under the eleven cooperative agreements. Some 750 American and about the same number of Soviet specialists were exchanged annually after the initial startup period, usually for one- to two-week visits to consult on work being performed in each country under the agreements.

This was largely an effort of the federal government rather than the private sector, and S & T exchanges with the Soviet Union, unlike cultural and educational exchanges, have remained government conducted and funded.

The U.S. motivation was primarily political, within the détente framework—to develop patterns of cooperation and interdependence which would hopefully lead to shared interests and more moderate behavior on the part of the Soviet Union. Secondary U.S. objectives were to use S & T exchanges to help solve practical scientific problems, and to gain increased access to the Soviet science community and learn what it was doing.

The Soviet motivation was to acquire U.S. science and technology which would be useful to Soviet economic—and military—development.

The topics of the working groups reflected the national priorities of the two countries where there was a convergent interest. Although the United States is generally considered to be ahead of the Soviet Union in most fields of S & T, the Soviet Union has much to offer in many fields where it is preeminent or even second best, and an attempt was made to balance the benefits. Even in fields where the United States is ahead, American scientists believed it would be useful to cooperate with the Soviets in order to learn how they approach various scientific problems. And the similarities in scale of the two countries, it was thought, would provide useful data and experience in solving common problems. Finally, there is some "geographic dependent" research of interest to American scientists that can be performed only in the Soviet Union.

Like all other exchanges with the Soviet Union, there was a break-in period during which problems developed which raised questions about the utility of some of the projects under the agreements.

Among these were difficulties in access to Soviet research, travel restrictions for Americans in the Soviet Union, questions about the mutual benefits of some research, Soviet efforts to learn as much as possible about U.S. research while giving as little as possible in return, administrative difficulties in working with the Soviet bureaucracy and questions about the cost effectiveness of the research. With regard to the last, no additional funds had been allocated to the federal agencies involved in the cooperative research—only the National Science Foundation has a "line item" in its budget for Soviet exchanges—and most of the joint research had to be funded from existing budgets. The bottom line question for many U.S. project managers, therefore, was whether the results were worth the costs.

A reassessment of the cooperative agreements began in the last year of the Carter administration when more cooperative research projects were terminated than initiated. U.S. lead agencies began to evaluate individual projects more strictly on their scientific merits, rather than as a means of continuing exchanges with the Soviet Union. More emphasis was placed on mutuality of benefits.

At the Carter-Brezhnev Vienna summit in 1979, unlike previous summits, there was no focus on exchanges and no new cooperative agreements were signed. On the U.S. side, there was recognition that the euphoria of détente was over, that there were a number of problem areas in scientific cooperation yet to be resolved and that it would be better to digest what had already been signed, rather than to sign new agreements for mainly political purposes.

In planning for the summit, the Soviets had suggested that a new cultural agreement be signed at Vienna. Informal discussions between the two governments disclosed, however, that there were too many issues to be resolved, and it was decided not to rush into a new agreement merely to have something to sign at the summit.

Much of the S & T cooperation was curtailed in the early 1980s. After the Soviet invasion of Afghanistan, the Carter administration suspended high-level meetings with the Soviets and ordered a full review of all cooperative projects. As a consequence, meetings of joint committees to review work under the cooperative agreements were suspended, and activity under the agreements declined as projects of marginal value to the United States were discontinued.

The Reagan administration, after martial law was imposed in Poland, took further action against three of the cooperative agreements—Science and Technology, Space and Energy—allowing them to lapse. An extension of the Transportation agreement was discussed by the two governments in the summer of 1983, but after the Soviet shootdown of the Korean airliner in September, this agreement was also allowed to lapse. By the end of 1983, the number of persons exchanged under the eleven cooperative agreements had fallen to about 20 percent of the 1979 level.

In the fundamental sciences, bilateral meetings between scientists of the two academies were suspended in 1980 after the Soviet invasion of Afghanistan and the exile of Andrei Sakharov, and the interacademy agreement was not renewed in 1982. Individual scientists continued to be exchanged between the academies, although at a much reduced level after the National Science Foundation cut the Academy's budget for exchanges with the Soviet Union by 45 percent in 1981. The U.S. and Soviet academies continued, nevertheless, to hold their biannual meetings on international security and arms control, reflecting the U.S. view that these talks were too important to suspend.

Human rights have also affected S & T exchanges with the Soviet Union. In the early 1980s, many U.S. scientists chose not to participate because of their concern over Soviet human rights violations, including the exile of Andrei Sakharov to Gorky, the imprisonment of Anatoly Shcharansky and Yuri Orlov, the misuse of psychiatry for political purposes and the decline in Jewish emigration.

The Reagan administration, although it sharply cut back exchanges with the Soviet Union during its first two years, argued that it was maintaining the structure of S & T exchanges so that they might be resumed when the political climate permitted. The agreement on atomic energy cooperation, for example, was renewed in August 1983, and cooperation was continued in areas of environmental protection, health and safety.

In mid-1986, seven of the original eleven cooperative agreements were still in effect. The four agreements which had not yet been renewed were in Transportation, Space, Energy, and Science and Technology.

The structure of S & T exchanges was indeed in place in November 1985 when the Reagan-Gorbachev summit signaled renewed interest in exchanges. It is evident, however, that the Reagan administration, in its first two years, was intent on dismantling the vestiges of détente, and a sharp cutback in S & T exchanges was one element of that policy.

President Reagan, in his 1982 report to the Congress on the U.S. government's international activities in science and technology, summed up the difficulties in exchanges with the Soviet Union.[1]

It is easy to imagine, the President said, the problems that might be solved by the cooperative efforts of the world's two largest scientific establishments. But these hopes, continued Mr. Reagan, come up against the following stark realities: many of the best Soviet scientific institutions are off-limits to foreigners, free exchange is inhibited because Soviet scientists face imprisonment for disclosure of unpublished research, Soviet scientists are not allowed to travel freely to scientific conferences abroad and many of the Soviet national conferences are closed to Western scientists, Jewish scientists face limited careers, and the Soviet government has chosen to imprison, exile or deny work to some of its most distinguished scientists, while others are sent to psychiatric hospitals in a flagrant misuse of science in service to the state.

None of these conditions in the Soviet Union had changed by November 1985 when the Geneva summit signaled a new start in U.S.-USSR exchanges.

Andrei Sakharov was still in exile in Gorky and the Soviet Army was still in Afghanistan when the National Academy of Sciences and the Soviet Academy of Sciences signed a new agreement on April 1, 1986, renewing their cooperation. The decision to sign the new agreement reflected the National Academy's view that its five-year boycott of Soviet exchanges was not working, and that U.S. scientists could better press their views on Sakharov's exile and other Soviet human rights violations by resuming relations with Soviet scientists.

The new agreement between the two academies provides for annual meetings of officers of the academies in which ". . . consideration will be given to steps which can be taken by the Academies to contribute to a favorable environment for scientific cooperation," an apparent reference to human rights.[2]

In an apparent response to criticism from within the National Academy, National Academy President Frank Press sent a telegram to Soviet Academy President A. P. Aleksandrov on April 9, one week after signing the new agreement, requesting the Soviet Academy's assistance in "bringing about a substantial amelioration of the situation of Academician Andrei Sakharov." The telegram, the text of which was released by the National Academy, notes that Sakharov is a member of the National Academy and that efforts on his behalf would improve the climate for scientific exchange and cooperation between the two academies.

Despite temporary political setbacks, Soviet-American S & T cooperation is likely to continue and to expand in the coming years. Although there will always be difficulties in cooperating with the Soviets, the overall attitude toward these exchanges on the part of the U.S. scientific community—both governmental and private—is positive.

Concern over the issue of mutual benefits and technology transfer under the eleven cooperative agreements with the Soviet Union prompted the Congress in 1982 to request the Department of State to report on the exchanges conducted under the agreements, including an assessment of the risk of transfer of militarily significant technology.

The State Department report, submitted on June 8, 1983, concluded that, while the benefits varied under the individual agreements, the United States tended to benefit from the exchange of information at least as much, if not more, than the Soviet Union.

The exchanges and other activities conducted under the agreements, the report added, "rarely involve the risk of the transfer of militarily significant technology," because most of the activities "are in basic research areas or involve scientific applications in the fields of health, safety or environmental protection." The intelligence community, the report continued, routinely assesses the risk of technology transfer, and "in those few instances where risk of technology transfer is identified, the activities are either cancelled or appropriately recast to minimize or eliminate such risk."[3]

A National Academy of Sciences report in 1977 cited the value of exchanges in giving the United States a more accurate assessment of the strengths and weaknesses of Soviet science. Commenting on U.S. overreaction to the Soviet launch of its Sputnik satellite in 1957, the report noted that many Americans were convinced that the Soviet Union had overtaken the United States in the physical sciences and engineering. The report concluded:

> The myth of the superiority of Soviet science would not have spread so far if scientific contacts with the Soviet Union before 1957 had not been so few. Lack of contact has led, at least on occasion, to exaggeration and unsound speculation. The reduction of these is one important achievement of the interacademy exchange program.[4]

The Cultural Factor

Often overlooked in evaluating S & T exchanges is the cultural or human factor, the effect on a Soviet scientist, indeed on all Soviet citizens, of a visit to the United States.

A former U.S. science attache in Moscow, John M. Joyce, notes that in the basically conservative Soviet society "the most outward looking people, the people most susceptible to external influence, are the scientists." Joyce adds that they are more likely to be advocates of change in the Soviet Union. As examples, he recalls that many of the most influential Soviet dissidents—Andrei Sakharov, Aleksander Lerner and Yuri Orlov—are scientists, and that five of the ten members of the Moscow Helsinki Watch Committee were scientists.[5]

Zhores Medvedev, an eminent Soviet scientist now living in Great Britain, believes that Soviet scientists have been the interpreters of the outside world for the Soviet Union:

> During 60 years of a new social system, science and scientists have provided the main links between Soviet society and the outside world because only for science were these links absolutely essential for survival. It is quite clear that these links will be more important in the future and scientific cooperation will provide the basis for cooperation at all other levels. Science, besides the part it played in the internal development of a very large, mostly self-sufficient, and very suspicious country, represented its eyes, ears, and all other senses in its interaction with the outside world, and explained it to other population groups, including the ruling political elite. This social function of science within a semi-closed society is extremely important, and it will become more so when there is better international cooperation.[6]

As for the importance of Soviet engineers and technologists, a look at any list of leading Soviet government and party officials will disclose that most of them, by training, are engineers of one kind or another.

Given their importance in Soviet society, it would appear to be in the U.S. interest to assist Soviet scientists and technologists in gaining a better understanding of the West, and the United States in particular. Properly conducted exchange and cooperative agreements, with adequate safeguards for technology transfer, provide the most effective way to do this.

A visit to the United States for Soviet citizens is a revelation. They are amazed by the high standard of living, the efficiency, the access by private citizens to institutions and officials, the freedom of choice, and they make the inevitable comparisons with the Soviet Union. The more perceptive Soviet visitors realize that most of what they have been taught about the United States is false. What they have accepted without question in the past, they will subject to scrutiny in the future. The effects in the Soviet Union will be long lasting.

Notes

1. "Message to Congress on the International Activities of the U.S. Government in Science and Technology," *Public Papers of the Presidents of the United States, Ronald Reagan*, vol. 1, 1982 (Washington, D.C.: U.S. Government Printing Office, 1983), pp. 341–344.

2. "Agreement on Scientific Cooperation Between the National Academy of Sciences of the USA and the Academy of Sciences of the USSR," Article 1, para. 1 (Washington, D.C.: National Academy of Sciences, 1986).

3. The State Department report was not published, but a summary of it may be found in "Are U.S.-Soviet Scientific and Technical Exchanges Worthwhile?" report no. G-332(a), August 10, 1983, Friends Committee on National Legislation, Washington, D.C.

4. *Review of U.S.-U.S.S.R. Interacademy Exchanges and Relations* (Washington, D.C.: National Academy of Sciences, 1977), p. 8.

5. John M. Joyce, "U.S.-Soviet Science Exchanges: A Foot In The Soviet Door," in "Soviet Science and Technology: Eyewitness Accounts" Seminar (Cambridge: Harvard University Russian Research Center, 1981).

6. Zhores A. Medvedev, *Soviet Science* (New York: W. W. Norton, 1978), pp. 204–205.

8

Sports and Tourism

Sports

American and Soviet athletes compete in a wide range of bilateral competitions including basketball, boxing, hockey, swimming and track and field, to name some of the more active ones. The total number of persons involved each year is difficult to assess because the U.S. national governing body for each sport deals directly with its Soviet counterpart, but several hundred persons from each country are believed to participate yearly.

Until 1963, each bilateral athletic competition was arranged through the two governments and was listed in the cultural agreement. Since 1964, the two governments have left the negotiations to their sports bodies, and the cultural agreement has included only general language endorsing sports exchanges.

The Soviets place a high priority on participating in, and winning, international athletic competitions, especially when the United States is their competitor. A victory over an American team, in whatever activity, gives the Soviets a psychological boost and helps them feel that they have arrived and been recognized as coequal, if not superior, to the United States.

The Soviets also use athletic victories as evidence that "socialism" is the superior system and will inevitably triumph over capitalism. This inevitability, of course, is backed up by generous government funding and extensive national training programs. The Soviets disapprove of professionalism in athletics, but Soviet athletes who represent their country abroad are, in fact, professionals, although they compete as amateurs.

Other Soviet motivations for athletic competitions with the United States include the reward value of a tour of the United States for their athletes and, in some sports, the financial gains to the Soviet state.

Winning is everything to the Soviets, and Soviet officials in international competitions have a reputation for favoring Soviet athletes in their close calls. This was so flagrant at the 1980 Moscow Olympics, where the home team provided the officials, that officials from foreign countries were used at the Los Angeles Olympics in 1984, even though this increased the costs to the organizers.

American teams are eager to compete with the Soviets in all sports. The two countries are evenly matched in many sports, and the Soviets have been improving rapidly as a result of their national training programs. Bilateral sports competitions draw good crowds in both countries.

Sports and politics do not mix, say the Soviets, and they were very bitter over U.S. withdrawal from the Moscow Olympics in 1980 after the Soviet invasion of Afghanistan. In this regard, however, they are overlooking their own record.

The Soviets cancelled several track meets with the United States during the late 1960s in protest against U.S. involvement in Vietnam. They have refused to participate, for political reasons, in world championships in countries such as Israel, Chile and South Korea. They threatened to boycott the 1968 Olympics if South Africa were permitted to participate, and they withdrew from the 1984 Olympics in Los Angeles with the phony charge that security for their athletes would be inadequate. They refused to permit participation by teams from Israel, South Africa and South Korea at the Goodwill Games, held in Moscow in 1986. And for 1988, when the Olympics are to be held in South Korea, they are exerting pressure to hold some of the events in North Korea as well.

The United States, however, has also mixed sports with politics. The Carter administration in 1980 pressured the U.S. Olympic team to withdraw from the Moscow Olympic games, and several U.S. sports competitions with the Soviet Union were cancelled in the wake of the shootdown of the Korean airliner in September 1983.

Bilateral sports exchanges between the two countries continued, however, between 1980 and 1985 when there was no cultural agreement, and they are likely to continue no matter how the political relationship between the two governments evolves.

This would appear to be one area in which governmental intrusion should be kept to a minimum.

Tourism

An estimated 80,000 to 100,000 American tourists visited the Soviet Union in calendar year 1985. By contrast, only 2,216 Soviet tourists visited the United States in Fiscal Year 1985.

The figures for the Americans are estimates, by the State Department, because only the Soviets know the exact number. The figure for the Soviets should be exact because it is the number of U.S. tourist visas issued to Soviet citizens for that year. Many of the Soviets, however, came on familial visits, with the costs paid by their U.S. relatives, and it is not known how many were actual tourists who came to see the United States. The statistics, however, whether exact or not, indicate the relatively low level of tourist traffic between the two countries, and the imbalance between Americans and Soviets.

The Department of Commerce, in 1974, had predicted that American tourists to the Soviet Union would number 230,000 to 300,000 by 1980, and twice that number by 1985, given a favorable political climate. These hopes were dashed by the unforeseen political events which soured U.S.-USSR relations.

Tourism has been encouraged in all cultural agreements since 1959, reflecting the interest in people-to-people contact—the "bridge-building" of the Eisenhower administration—as well as the interests of the U.S. and Soviet travel industries.

An American Express travel office was opened in Moscow in 1958 following signature of the first agreement, and a Soviet Intourist office in New York the same year. Direct air service between the two countries began in 1968, and the flow of American tourists to the Soviet Union took off, reaching more than 100,000 in 1978.

Soviet tourist travel to the United States has been much smaller. During the 1960s there were a few groups each year, but the total number of Soviet tourists to the United States never reached more than a few hundred. In 1969, for example, only 165 Soviet tourists came to the United States, while 20,000 Americans went to the Soviet Union.

One limiting factor has been the reluctance of the Soviet government to spend its much-needed hard currency on tourist travel to the West. However, with the start of flights to the United States in 1968 by Aeroflot, the Soviet airline, the Soviets could pay in rubles for their travel to the United States.

With détente, there was a sharp increase in Soviet visitors to the United States for official, business and exchange travel, but not for tourism. Some Soviet citizens, however, were permitted to visit relatives in the United States, with their U.S. hosts paying all costs. The number of such family visits reached 2,283 in 1979, before declining to 1,423 in 1983.

To further encourage tourism, a U.S.-USSR Tourism Committee was established in 1974. The Committee met regularly to consider proposals to facilitate tourism in both directions. The United States, in 1976, proposed an agreement on tourism between the two governments —an example of the agreement mania of the détente years—primarily to encourage more visits by Soviet tourists. This proposal, however, fell victim to the cooling of relations following the Jackson-Vanik amendment and the failure to liberalize trade between the two countries.

Political events then intervened to bring about a decline in tourist travel in both directions. The Carter administration's boycott of the 1980 Moscow Olympics and its forced reduction in the number of Aeroflot flights to the United States were serious blows to tourism between the two countries. A further blow was the Reagan administration's 1981 embargo of all direct bilateral air and maritime travel between the United States and the Soviet Union and Poland, in response to the Soviet role in the imposition of martial law in Poland. The final blow was the 1983 embargo against direct business between U.S. air carriers and Aeroflot, as well as the closing of Aeroflot offices in the United States, imposed by the Reagan administration in 1983 after the Soviet shootdown of the Korean airliner. One result of the latter move was to prohibit U.S. carriers from accepting tickets written on Aeroflot ticket stock.

These U.S. actions did not have a major effect on American tourist travel to the Soviet Union since Americans were able to travel via West European carriers. Soviet travelers to the United States, however, had to be routed through either Montreal or Mexico City via Aeroflot which had limited capacity to North America. Moreover, Soviet travelers had to have tickets from another carrier for the final leg of their travel to the United States.

Does tourism really matter? It can be argued that U.S. tourist travel to the Soviet Union helps the Soviet Union to earn hard currency and adds to the U.S. trade deficit, but does little to help Americans to understand the Soviet Union.

Tours conducted by Intourist, the Soviet state travel monopoly, are generally limited to the larger cities of the Soviet Union, and they do little to facilitate contact with Soviet citizens. Intourist guides—often the only Soviet citizens an American tourist gets to meet—offer boiler plate responses to questions about the Soviet Union. It might be said of tourism in the Soviet Union, with apologies to Lord Chesterfield, that the travel restrictions are ridiculous, the pleasures dubious and the expense damnable.

The experienced and sophisticated traveler, however, can learn much about the Soviet Union from a short visit, particularly if he or she is a little adventurous, willing to depart from the standard Intourist tour of museums and sites, and tries, instead, to see how Soviet citizens live. Visits to food shops, department stores, farmer's markets, parks and other places where Soviet citizens throng can provide much information about how they live. And with or without some knowledge of the Russian language, there are possibilities for encounters with Soviet citizens. Considering how little information about the Soviet Union is available to American citizens, travel to the Soviet Union, even under Intourist's restrictive conditions, can help to increase American understanding of that society.

American tourists interested in meeting Soviet citizens should consider the programs offered by U.S. travel agencies and private organizations for study tours of the Soviet Union for professionals, students and avocational groups which bring American visitors into direct contact with Soviet citizens who have similar interests.

The Soviet Union also seeks to bring its tourists to the United States into contact with American citizens, and to arrange meetings with local organizations in order to provide platforms for explaining Soviet government policies.

These Soviet tourist groups are organized by the USSR Committee on Friendship with Other Countries, commonly called "Friendship House" from the building in Moscow where it is housed. Such tourist groups are usually organized around the professions or ethnic groups, but they always include a few newspaper people or scholars from the Academy research institutes who are experienced spokespersons for Soviet policies.

During the 1970s, meetings between these tourist groups and Americans in the cities they visited were often arranged by local chapters of the National Council of American-Soviet Friendship, a U.S. organization. The Soviet Embassy in Washington, however, was unhappy with these meetings because they were often with U.S. groups of little importance in their communities, and the Embassy asked the State Department for assistance in arranging meetings with mainstream American groups.

Tourism between the two countries can be expected to increase in future years—including Soviet tourism to the United States—if political relations stay on a steady course. It is in the U.S. interest to see that tourists to both countries depart as much as possible from the standard tours and come into contact with citizens of the host country through home visits and meetings with citizen groups. Unfortunately, tourists in both countries usually visit only the very large cities rather than the "heartland."

Soviet visitors to the United States usually ask to see New York, Washington, D.C., Chicago, San Francisco and Los Angeles, because these correspond, in their view, to Moscow, Leningrad, Kiev and a few other large cities. Other smaller U.S. cities are considered provincial, as they would be in the Soviet Union.

This was illustrated by a high ranking Soviet official who came to the United States in the 1970s. With some reluctance he agreed to add Houston and Minneapolis to his itinerary. When asked, at the end of his visit, how he found the United States, he replied that he was very impressed by our "provincial cities."

9

Problems in Exchanges

More problems in Soviet exchanges? Unfortunately, there are some, in addition to those already mentioned, which are so pervasive, and indeed endemic to the Soviet system, that they apply virtually to all exchanges with the Soviet Union and are experienced not only by the United States but by all countries.

Visas

Without visas there would be no exchanges. Soviet citizens need an American visa to enter the United States, and U.S. citizens need a Soviet visa to enter the Soviet Union.

The denial of a visa can, and often does, delay or force cancellation of an exchange. This is annoying for would-be travelers as well as for officials who must authorize, or not authorize, the visas. The Soviet Union is the major culprit, but the United States is not completely blameless in this regard.

Anyone who has visited the Soviet Union knows the frustrations in obtaining a Soviet visa. The application must be submitted well in advance of departure. The prospective visitor either must have an invitation from a Soviet institution, be a participant in an official exchange or travel via Intourist with all costs paid in advance. The visa is often issued shortly before departure, but there is no assurance that it will indeed be issued.

When a visa is denied, it can be assumed that the applicant has done something in the past to displease the Soviets, usually on a previous visit to the Soviet Union. This may have been an actual transgression of Soviet law or something not illegal, such as contact with dissidents.

Visas have been denied because of something an applicant has published on the Soviet Union, as some U.S. scholars have learned to their regret. And visas are issued at the last minute because that's how the Soviet bureaucracy works.

The United States has also denied visas. These denials are based on the Immigration and Nationality Act of 1952 (McCarran-Walter) as amended, which designates categories of aliens who are ineligible to receive visas and are excluded from admission to the United States.[1] Section 212 (a) 28 of the Act has been used most frequently to find Soviets ineligible, but Sections 212 (a) 27 and 29 are also used when more serious grounds for exclusion exist.

Paragraph 28 pertains to aliens who are current or former members of the communist party of a foreign state or any organization "that advocates the economic, international and governmental doctrines of world communism." Paragraph 27 concerns aliens who seek to enter the United States "to engage in activities which would be prejudicial to the public interest, or endanger the welfare, safety, or security of the United States." Paragraph 29 applies to aliens who, after entry would probably "engage in activities which would be prohibited by the laws of the United States relating to espionage, sabotage, public disorder, or in other activity subversive to the national security."

Soviet applicants for visas under exchange programs normally do not apply personally at a U.S. consulate in the Soviet Union. Their visa applications are forwarded to the American Consul through the USSR Ministry of Foreign Affairs. Since applicants cannot be interviewed by the Consul, the normal procedure to determine their admissibility under the Act, they are automatically presumed to be inadmissable under paragraph 28 as a member of an organization which advocates "world communism."

To facilitate U.S. visa issuance for Soviet citizens travelling under exchange programs, procedures were worked out in the late 1950s under which the State Department may recommend that the Attorney General grant a waiver of visa ineligibility and admit them to the United States temporarily. Such waivers have been routinely granted for Soviet citizens found ineligible under Section 212 (a) 28.

The McGovern Amendment to the Act further facilitated the approval of waivers of visa ineligibility for routine cases under Section 212 (a) 28. Sponsored by Sen. George McGovern and passed in 1977, it requires the Department of State to recommend a waiver of visa ineligibility in virtually all Section 212 (a) 28 cases. Consequently, a determination of ineligibility under 27 or 29 is now the principal basis for visa denial to a prospective Soviet exchange visitor, since ineligibility under these sections of the Act cannot be waived.

The Soviets, for various reasons, also deny visas to some U.S. citizens. Denial of a Soviet visa to a member of a U.S. delegation due to depart for the Soviet Union creates a dilemma for other delegation members. Should they accept the Soviet decision and leave their colleague behind? Or should that show a united front and cancel the visit or postpone it until the visa is issued? The decision, of course, is up to each delegation, but pressure on the Soviet host institution in the exchange has been known to work. If the Soviet inviting institution has sufficient clout and wants the exchange to proceed as scheduled, the decision to deny the visa can sometimes be reversed. Unfortunately, a visa denial usually occurs at the last minute, making it difficult for the Americans to change their travel plans, and for the Soviets to reconsider their decision.

The visa "game" is not pleasant for officials who administer exchanges. At times, one side or the other has chosen to retaliate for a visa denial by taking reciprocal action. In cases of American scholars who have been denied Soviet visas because of something they have written about the Soviet Union, the State Department, with the concurrence of IREX, has denied visas to Soviet scholars, and such actions have caused the Soviets to reconsider their turndowns.

There is no simple solution to the visa problem. It will exist as long as governments are bound by specific legislation denying admission to certain categories of aliens, or feel obliged to keep out people whose writings or views they do not like.

Access and Travel

It has long been an American tradition to show foreign visitors what they want to see in the United States and to have them meet with anyone willing to see them. In fact, it has been traditional that foreign leaders invited to the United States under the U.S. government's International Visitor Program can write their own program and itinerary.

Soviet official visitors to the United States have asked to see and been given tours of depressed areas of our big cities. Meetings have been arranged with opponents as well as supporters of the administration, and with some Americans who might even be called dissidents. Americans like to show their country, warts and all. Moreover, the entire territory of the United States is open to Soviet visitors under exchange programs.

Not so in the Soviet Union where there is a "Potemkin village" tradition, and the authorities want foreign visitors to see the Soviet Union as the party and its ideology say it is supposed to be, rather than as it actually is. Soviet citizens who are out of favor with the regime are not easily available to visiting Americans. Visitors are given upbeat briefings on how well everything is going, replete with endless statistics on how the current plan is being fulfilled.

A delegation of U.S. state governors was given this treatment once in Ukraine where a high Soviet official subjected them to a long talk on how well everything was going in his republic. The American governors, no novices to the demands of political office, finally asked if there were any problems. The Soviet official's reply that there were no problems was greeted with incredulous laughter.

This is changing as a new generation of Soviet officials slowly comes on the scene, with more experience in handling foreign visitors and more confidence about acknowledging Soviet shortcomings. But the programs and itineraries prepared for foreign visitors are not going to show Soviet problems or include visits with those who do not have regime approval. Such visits can be arranged, with silent acquiescence by the authorities. But independent writers, scholars and scientists, as well as dissidents, will not be invited to official meetings with foreign visitors.

Much of the Soviet Union is still closed to travel by foreign visitors, and open areas are often closed "for reasons of a temporary nature," meaning that no foreign visitors are wanted there at that time. This too is unlikely to change in the near future.

Contacts between Soviet citizens and foreigners have been further limited by recent Soviet legislation. As a result of 1984 amendments to the law of December 25, 1958, "On Criminal Liability for Crimes Against the State," Soviet citizens face the possibility of criminal charges if they provide virtually any kind of information to a foreigner without official authorization.[2] Specifically, the new law broadens the definition of treason to include acts threatening state security, and it defines "state secret" to include the concept of "work-related secret." The amendments to the law reflect the traditional Soviet view that all information about the Soviet Union is a state secret unless it has been officially approved for release. It is bound to have a restraining effect on contacts of Soviet citizens with foreign scholars, scientists, journalists and others.

Despite the difficulties of access and travel, foreign visitors can have a useful and informative stay if they know what and whom they want to see, and they make their requests to their Soviet hosts politely but firmly. The Soviet first response is likely to be "nyet," but if a request is repeated again and again, and the Soviet hosts find that the visitor is serious about a request, it may be filled. There are indeed many things the Soviets do not want to show to a foreign visitor, but more often they simply don't want to take the trouble to change a prearranged itinerary once it has been approved by higher authorities and the necessary travel and hotel reservations have been made.

Name Requests

It is a long established procedure in U.S.-USSR exchanges that the sending side nominates those whom it sends to the other country. The Soviets, however, do not always send their best people on exchanges. It is often the second best, or even second-raters, who are sent abroad. The best person in a particular field may not have clearance for foreign travel, may allegedly be privy to state secrets, may be Jewish or considered a possible defector. Whatever the reason, it is a disappointment for the U.S. side in an exchange to know that it has sent the leading Americans in their field, but the Soviets have not sent their best.

It is understandable, therefore, that many Americans have sought to invite individual Soviets, by name, to visit the United States, what is known as a "name request" in exchange parlance. The invitation may result from a personal acquaintance with a Soviet scientist or scholar, or knowledge of his or her preeminence. There is evidence that the Soviets are slowly moving in this direction.

National Academy of Sciences President Frank Press stated in 1983, for example, that any new agreement with the Soviet Academy of Sciences must include the principle "that each Academy can invite scientists from the other country and that they will be included in the exchange program."[3] And when the new agreement between the two academies was signed in April 1986, it included language providing that candidates for exchange may be invited "through the sending Academy by the receiving Academy" in addition to the quota set forth in the agreement, and "it is desirable that such visits become an important and significant portion of the total individual exchanges."[4]

Under the Fulbright Lecturer Exchange, the Soviets, since the mid-1970s, have agreed that U.S. universities may name the Soviet professors they wish to host as lecturers, and in many cases the Soviets have sent the requested lecturers. This procedure was written into the 1985 cultural agreement which specifies that the two governments will exchange lecturers "in accordance with the wishes of the sending and receiving sides."[5]

The general rule for most other exchanges, however, is that the sending side decides whom it will send.

Decisions, Delays and No-Shows

The long lead time required by the Soviet Union to plan exchanges and to make decisions is another frustration for Americans seeking to expand contacts. The Soviets do not answer letters or telegrams promptly, if at all. The best, but not the cheapest, way to get a decision from Moscow officials, as many Americans have learned, is to go there and meet with them personally, preferably over food and drink.

Decisions are not made easily by the Soviet bureaucracy, particularly if they concern the United States. The smallest questions frequently have to be bucked to a higher authority for decision, and at each step some official may be reluctant to accept responsibility.

Once a decision has been made and the dates set for a conference or visit, there are often postponements or cancellations, sometimes at the last minute, with great disappointment and inconvenience for the U.S. hosts. On numerous occasions the U.S. side has been informed, only the day before a scheduled arrival, that a Soviet visitor has had to postpone.

Yuri Lyubimov, the celebrated Soviet theater director, for example, was due to arrive in the United States in the late 1970s, after repeated U.S. invitations to him had been turned down by the Ministry of Culture with the excuse that he had other commitments. One day before his scheduled arrival date, the Soviet Embassy in Washington called me to report that the visit had been postponed. In 1984, Lyubimov failed to return to the Soviet Union from a stay in the West and was fired from his position as director of Moscow's prestigious Taganka Theater.

The Soviets also have difficulty preparing papers in advance of a conference. In many bilateral meetings, each side customarily prepares a paper which is sent to the other side in advance. The Americans usually submit their papers on time. Soviet papers are often not submitted at all, arrive too late to be useful or contain little of substance. This represents a longstanding Soviet tactic to have the other side speak first before they disclose their own position. This too is unlikely to change.

Human Rights

Most Americans are concerned about violations of human rights in the Soviet Union—the exile of Andrei Sakharov, the misuse of psychiatry for political purposes, the harassment of religious and ethnic groups, the persecution of independent writers, anti-Semitism and restrictions on emigration.

U.S. views on human rights have been made known in statements by Presidents Carter and Reagan, in bilateral talks with the Soviets, in the Congress and the press and in multilateral forums such as the United Nations and the Conference on Security and Cooperation in Europe (CSCE). And some Americans have made their views known by calling for a boycott or suspension of exchanges with the Soviet Union.

Among those urging a suspension have been prominent scientists who otherwise would be strong supporters of exchanges. In protest against the exile of Andrei Sakharov and the arrest and imprisonment of other Soviet scientists, some American scientists have urged a suspension of science exchanges with the Soviet Union.

At the CSCE Scientific Forum, held in Hamburg in 1980 only weeks after Sakharov's exile, protests were voiced against the exile of Sakharov and Soviet practices restricting scientific exchange. The Report of the Forum, approved by all thirty-five participating nations including the Soviet Union, states that "respect for human rights and fundamental freedoms by all states represents one of the foundations for a significant improvement of their mutual relations, and of international scientific cooperation at all levels." The Report also calls for "equitable opportunities for scientific research and for wider communication and travel necessary for professional purposes."[6]

It can be argued that the Soviets don't observe such statements they have signed, and regarding human rights this is certainly true. Nevertheless, when the Soviets agree to such a statement, it is on the record, and it provides the basis for Western scientists to raise the issue whenever they meet with the Soviets. Western perseverance in obtaining Soviet concurrence to statements and agreements on human rights will not radically change the situation in the Soviet Union. Such efforts should be seen as small steps designed to help bring the Soviet Union into the modern world.

One argument for continuing exchanges is that through exchanges many Soviet violations of human rights have become known in the West. Exchanges are also used to carry Western human rights protests to the Soviet Union. At meetings with Soviets, Americans can and do raise these issues, thus ensuring that the Soviets understand the strong feelings in the West on their violations of basic human rights.

Notes

1. 8 U.S.C. 1101.

2. The amendments to the 1958 law were approved by the USSR Supreme Soviet Presidium and signed by Andropov on January 11, 1984.

3. *Overview of International Science and Technology Policy,* Hearings

Before the Subcommittees on International Security and Scientific Affairs, Committee on Foreign Affairs, House of Representatives, August 2, 1983 (Washington, D.C.: U.S. Government Printing Office, 1983), p. 61.

4. "Agreement on Scientific Cooperation Between the National Academy of Sciences of the USA and the Soviet Academy of Sciences of the USSR," Article 5, para. 20 (Washington, D.C.: National Academy of Sciences, 1986).

5. See Article 1, para. 1b of the Agreement in Appendix B.

6. *The Helsinki Forum and East-West Scientific Exchange* , Joint Hearing before two subcommittees of the Committee on Foreign Affairs, U.S. House of Representatives and the Commission on Security and Cooperation in Europe (Washington, D.C.: U.S. Government Printing Office, 1980), p. 221.

10

From Geneva to Geneva

Introduction

From the Geneva Foreign Ministers meeting of 1955 to the Geneva summit meeting of 1985, via Helsinki and Madrid, is a circular route that will help to assess the results of twenty-eight years of Soviet-American cultural exchanges.

Assessing the results of cultural exchanges with the Soviet Union is not easy. How are changes in attitudes measured in a country which does not permit foreigners to commission public opinion polls? And how much of the change that has occurred there since the death of Stalin can be attributed to Western influences, or to strictly internal Soviet developments? All U.S. proposals for joint studies of exchanges have been rejected by the Soviets, and until they are accepted, only the U.S. side of exchanges can be studied.

What can be measured, however, are changes made by the Soviet Union to accommodate exchanges with the West—changes made either as a result of having signed cultural agreements or resulting from pressure by the West. From these changes, we can learn how far the West has come in its exchanges with the Soviet Union, and how far it still has to go.

The 1955 Geneva Conference

Cultural exchange between East and West on the intergovernmental level had its origins in the seventeen-point proposal made at the 1955 Geneva Foreign Ministers Conference which was discussed earlier in this study.[1]

Soviet Foreign Minister V. M. Molotov rejected the Western proposals and charged the West with interference in Soviet internal affairs. Subsequently, however, the Soviet Union acquiesced in many of the Western proposals, either in the cultural and scientific agreements it signed with the West, or by actions it took unilaterally. These changes may seem marginal today by Western standards, but by opening Soviet borders ever so slightly to Western influence, they represent major departures in Soviet policy.

The Soviets have acquiesced, since 1955, in full or in part, in the following Western proposals (the numbers used at Geneva are used below):

3. exchange of official periodicals—the Soviets, in 1956, agreed to exchange monthly periodicals, *Amerika* and *Soviet Life*;
5. increase the exchange of government publications—this has been done progressively over the years;
6. sale of Western films to the Soviet Union—begun in 1958, but sales have been limited;
7. exchange of exhibitions—begun in 1959 and continued each year;
11. increase in tourism—Western tourism to the Soviet Union has greatly increased; Soviet tourism to the West has begun, but on a very limited basis;
12. exchanges of persons in the professions, culture, science and technology—begun in 1958;
13. facilitate attendance at international congresses—begun in 1958;
14. exchange of cultural and sporting events—begun in 1958;
15. exchanges of students—begun in 1958;
17. direct air transport between countries—direct air service between the United States and the Soviet Union began in 1968, was terminated by the United States in 1981 and was resumed in 1986.

Proposals which have been implemented in part:

4. exchanges of books, periodicals and newspapers between libraries, universities and professional and scientific bodies, and for general and unimpeded sale to the public—the first part has been implemented, but not the second;
9. exchange of monthly uncensored broadcasts on world developments—the Soviets agreed, in the 1985 cultural agreement, to exchanges of television broadcasts, but this has not yet been implemented;
10. end censorship of outgoing press despatches, and end denial to journalists of access to normal sources of information—the first part was implemented in 1961.

Proposals which have not been implemented:

1. freer exchange of information and ideas, including an end to censorship;
2. opening of information centers in each other's capitals;
8. end jamming of radio broadcasts—Soviet jamming of the Voice of America ended partially in 1959 and completely in 1963, was resumed in 1968, ended again in 1973, and was resumed again in 1980; Radio Liberty and Radio Free Europe have been jammed consistently;
16. end travel restrictions on diplomats.

For those who like to keep score, and allowing one point for full implementation and a half point for partial, the United States has scored on eleven and one-half of the Western proposals since 1955, while striking out on five and one-half.

As an indication of possible further changes to come, Japan signed a cultural agreement with the Soviet Union in May 1986 in which the Soviet Union agreed, in principle, to permit Japan to open a cultural center in Moscow. Details, however, have yet to be agreed to.

The Helsinki Process

At the Conference on Security and Cooperation in Europe (CSCE), 1973–1975, twenty years after the Geneva Foreign Ministers Conference, the Western allies were again in Geneva, debating with the Soviet Union and its East European allies the same question which they had raised in 1955—how to provide for a freer exchange of people, information and ideas. And, as in 1955, the Soviets were countering with Molotov's charge of interference in their internal affairs.[2]

The major issues at the conference were military security and human rights, but also addressed were culture, education, information, science and technology, in the belief that exchanges and cooperation in these fields also contribute to security and cooperation.

There were two differences from 1955, however. First, all thirty-three European states—except Albania—plus Canada and the United States were participants at CSCE, and most of them, by 1975, had considerable experience in exchanges with the Soviet Union. They knew the problem areas and where improvements should be made. Second, exchanges had come of age and were recognized by all participants, including the Soviet Union and its allies, as a legitimate and useful element in bilateral relations.

After two years of negotiation, the Soviets agreed to a number of Western and neutral initiatives which were embodied in the Conference Final Act which was signed at Helsinki.[3] These include agreement to permit direct communication between institutions and persons involved in cultural exchanges, contacts between authors and their foreign publishers, dissemination of foreign books and published materials, and foreign travel by persons active in culture.

On education, it was agreed to encourage direct exchanges between universities and direct contacts between educators, to facilitate travel by scholars, teachers and students, and to encourage cooperation in the teaching of foreign languages.

On working conditions for foreign journalists, agreement was reached on improvements in visa issuance, procedures for travel within the host country, access to news sources, and transmission of news dispatches, tape recordings and film.

At the Madrid CSCE Review Meeting, 1980–1983, convened to review progress made since Helsinki, further agreements were hammered out.[4] These include the public sale and distribution of imported printed matter, and possibilities for the public to subscribe to foreign publications. For foreign journalists, further improvements were made in visa issuance, travel procedures, and establishing and maintaining personal contacts and communication with their news sources.

These may well be empty Soviet promises in the short run. When foreign relations are strained, the Soviets tighten up at home and tend to ignore commitments they have agreed to reluctantly. But when relations improve, some of these commitments are likely to be honored, particularly if the Soviets are pressed by other governments to do so. The process of normalizing communication with the Soviet Union is a long one, and it is important that Soviet agreement in these areas be on the public record.[5]

In the final analysis, however, the West must recognize that it can push the Soviets no farther than they are willing to go themselves on these issues at any particular time. The changes must come from within Soviet society.

The Europeanization of Russia

The Helsinki and Madrid agreements and the results of some thirty years of Soviet exchanges with the West should be seen, in the long run, as steps in the Europeanization of Russia, an historical process which began in the fifteenth century after Moscow asserted its independence from the Mongols.

Historians differ on the significance of Mongol rule on Russian history, but they agree that it effectively isolated Russia from Europe, and at a crucial time when Europe was entering a period of economic development. This isolation contributed to Russia's backwardness from which she has never fully recovered. As a consequence, the Renaissance and the Reformation, with their emphasis on the individual and free inquiry, never reached Russia. Mongol rule, moreover, contributed to Russia's legacies of autocratic rule, the subservience of the individual to the state, and a collective approach which have all served to differentiate Russia from Europe. Mongol rule did not make Russia Asian, but it did delay its becoming European.

The long process of Europeanization began when Ivan III brought Italian architects and engineers to Russia to build his Kremlin, palaces and cathedrals. It continued under Peter the Great and other tsars, selectively borrowing from the West, mainly in technology and administrative knowhow, but rejecting those Western ideas which Russia's leaders considered alien and subversive. This has not changed in our time.

The Soviet Union today has its own reasons for signing the Helsinki Accords. These include projecting a peaceful image, promoting trade and technological cooperation with the West, setting the stage for further arms reduction talks and ultimately replacing U.S. influence in Europe. But the Soviet Union today is also continuing Russia's historic process of Europeanization by asking that it formally be accepted as a member of the European club of states. However, while seeking recognition as a European state, the Soviet Union rejects the rules of the club's behavior—the human rights and humanitarian values that are basic to European culture.

In exchange for membership in the European club, the West has asked that Russia agree to abide by the rules of the club—to accept the human rights values of Europe as set forth in the Helsinki and Madrid documents, and to restore the free movement of people, information and ideas which has contributed so much to the cultural unity of Europe.

Change comes slowly to Russia, but change is inevitable. The West should encourage this change through the contacts and exchanges agreed to at Helsinki and Madrid, what has come to be known as the Helsinki process, or what might also be called the Europeanization of Russia.

Notes

1. The full text of the seventeen proposals may be found in Appendix A.

2. For a comprehensive analysis of the negotiation of the CSCE Final Act by a participant, see John J. Marcesa, *To Helsinki—The Conference on Security and Cooperation in Europe, 1973–1975* (Durham: Duke University Press, 1985).

3. "Conference on Security and Cooperation in Europe: Final Act," *Department of State Bulletin*, September 1, 1975, pp. 323–350.

4. *The Madrid Concluding Document, The Madrid CSCE Review Meeting,* Commission on Security and Cooperation in Europe, U.S. Congress, November 1983.

5. For an analysis of the results of the Madrid CSCE Conference by the head of the U.S. delegation, see Max M. Kampelman, "An Assessment of the Madrid CSCE Followup Conference, *Department of State Bulletin*, September 1, 1983, pp. 59–60.

11

The Reagan-Gorbachev Summit

Introduction

The long-awaited Reagan-Gorbachev summit meeting in Geneva in late November 1985 was the stage for signature of yet another cultural agreement between the two superpowers. This agreement reinstated many of the exchanges which had been suspended since 1980 after the Soviet invasion of Afghanistan, and it added several new ones.

Participants in summit meetings need documents to sign to indicate that the meetings are a success. Since there were no major agreements to sign at Geneva, the new cultural agreement received more than the passing attention usually accorded it.

The administration's intention to negotiate a cultural agreement with the Soviet Union was announced by President Reagan in an address on June 27, 1984, to participants in a Conference on U.S.-Soviet Exchanges, held at the Kennan Institute for Advanced Russian Studies in Washington, D.C. The offer to the Soviets on exchange negotiation was one of several steps, the President said, which were part of an effort to find ways ". . . to reach out and establish better communication with the people and the government of the Soviet Union" in an effort to reduce the threat and use of force in solving international disputes, reduce armaments and establish a better working relationship.[1]

Negotiations for the cultural agreement had been scheduled to start in Moscow in September 1983, but they were postponed, along with several other initiatives to improve Soviet-American relations, after the Soviet shootdown of Korean Airlines Flight 007.

When the negotiations finally did start, on August 8, 1984, they were to continue over an unprecedented fifteen months, during which the American and Soviet representatives met sixty-five times for more than 200 hours.[2] By comparison, the first cultural agreement, in 1958, had required three months to negotiate, while the third agreement, in 1962, had required five months, the previous record for length. In most other years, one or two weeks were required.

There are several possible explanations for the lengthy negotiations this time. First, there was no rush; neither side was pressed for time. Second, the negotiations were in Moscow, on Soviet home turf, where they usually take longer than in Washington. Moreover, the principal U.S. negotiator was an officer at the American Embassy, resident in Moscow. Neither side, therefore, was pressed to wrap things up quickly and return home. Third, there were several difficult issues—a Soviet request for "guarantees of security" for participants in exchanges, and U.S. requests for establishment of cultural centers in the two capitals, broadcasts by representatives of one country on the television of the other and, of course, the perennially difficult thematic exhibitions.

The Soviets rejected outright the request for cultural centers. The question of "guarantees of security" was resolved early in the negotiation, but there was disagreement over how this would be said in the Russian and English languages. The most difficult issues, over which there was prolonged discussion, were the U.S. requests for broadcasts by representatives of each country on the television of the other and, as in the past, the thematic exhibitions.

From the text of the agreed document, it is apparent that each delegation took a "maximalist" position, seeking, wherever possible, to commit the other to accept its draft language which spelled out, in detail, exactly how each exchange would be carried out. And, as the negotiations progressed and it became apparent that the agreement would be signed at the summit, each negotiator came under pressure to get the best possible document. Like many other U.S.-USSR negotiations, it became a test of will.

The 1985 Cultural Agreement

The 1985 agreement is the longest cultural agreement to date. With its two annexes, it is forty-one pages in length, typed double-space, while the previous agreement, in 1973, was thirty-two pages.

It seems that with the years, as new exchanges have been added, as cultural contacts between the two countries have expanded and as the role of the U.S. government has diminished, the agreement, instead of withering away—as many had initially hoped—has become more lengthy and more detailed, as each government has become more distrustful of the other and has sought to ensure that it is not bested in these exchanges.

Despite its length, the cultural agreement signed at the Geneva Summit on November 21, 1985, does not differ significantly from the previous agreement signed in Washington on June 19, 1973.[3] Changes in the cultural agreement have come slowly over the years, and there have seldom been radical departures from previous agreements.

In each negotiation, U.S. negotiators have sought to introduce new exchanges and to make improvements in existing ones, in an effort to break down barriers to free exchanges of ideas, information and people. Soviet negotiators, by contrast, have usually sought to retain the language of the previous agreement which has been cleared at the highest levels of the Soviet government. To make the slightest change in previously agreed language involves prolonged debate and delay on the Soviet side. Some of the changes in the 1985 agreement include:

- reciprocity and mutual benefit in exchanges are emphasized;
- wherever exchanges in science and technology are mentioned, they are balanced by also mentioning exchanges in culture and education, or the humanities and the social sciences;
- in Article I, new language has been added to ensure "the safety of, and normal working conditions for, those participating in American-Soviet exchanges"; this apparently is all the U.S. negotiators could give to meet the Soviet request for "guarantees of security";
- in Article IV (education), there is language calling for the exchange of "more young researchers preparing dissertations," an apparent reference to the long-standing Soviet desire to increase the Graduate Student/Young Faculty Exchange, and the U.S. desire to lower the age level of the Soviet participants;
- in Article VII (radio and television), there is new language providing for "Appearances of representatives of each country on television of the other country," a U.S. request, but this is followed by a standard Soviet escape clause, "in accordance with existing practices and regulations of each country";
- in Article VIII (books and publishing), there is reference to the desirability of "greater familiarity of each country's people with the literature and other publications of the other," another long-standing Soviet request, but this is somewhat balanced by agreement to have exchanges of book exhibits, in which both sides have a strong interest;
- in Article XV, there is new language providing for "the further development of contacts and cooperation between archival organizations of the two countries"; this reflects a long-standing

U.S. effort to gain access by U.S. scholars to Soviet archives, where access has always been difficult.

As in previous cultural agreements there is attached a "Program of Cooperation and Exchanges," with Annex, for the three-year period 1986–1988.[4] This Program and its Annex spell out, in excruciating and convoluted detail, exactly what will be exchanged under the various articles of the agreement, in how many numbers, and under what conditions, financial and otherwise.

The Program is where the Soviet penchant for numbers and long-range planning comes into play. But the Program is also important for the U.S. side, for it spells out which exchanges will be implemented and paid for by the U.S. government—important also for U.S. budget planners—and which exchanges will be carried out and paid for by the private sector. In the latter case, the U.S. government only "encourages" or "facilitates" an exchange. Among the more important changes in the new Program are:

- an increase in the exchange of university lecturers—under the Fulbright Program—from ten to fifteen each year from each country;
- new language to encourage the expansion of undergraduate exchanges in Russian and English language studies, but without specifying numbers;
- a new exchange of fifteen language teachers from each country at the secondary school level for six weeks each summer;
- the inclusion of language providing for the annual exchange of six language teachers from each country to teach in the other country's schools for a period of three months each year; this brings under the cultural agreement the previously existing non-official exchange conducted between the American Field Service and the USSR Ministry of Education;
- new language for exchanges of art exhibitions which provides for financial responsibilities of governments in case of loss, as well as immunity from seizure on the part of previous owners and adequate security for the exhibitions;
- the establishment of "close contacts" between the Main Archival Administration of the USSR and the National Archives of the United States;
- the expansion of exchanges of "young people, workers, farmers and representatives of other vocations," although it is not

specified who will conduct these exchanges, nor how many people will be exchanged and under what conditions.

While the changes cited above may seem trivial, and even inappropriate for two superpowers to negotiate, they do help to explain why it took fifteen months to negotiate the agreement. They also explain why some have questioned how we got ourselves into a situation where we exchange people "like sacks of grain," to use the expression of Robert F. Byrnes.[5]

The answer is that the Soviets require an intergovernmental agreement to conduct certain exchanges with the United States, and the U.S. government finds an agreement useful to ensure its cultural and educational programs in the Soviet Union. Without an agreement, the Soviets could be expected to take full advantage of our open society, while denying or limiting our access to theirs.

Reagan's People-to-People Initiatives

President Reagan, in his pre-summit address to the nation on November 14, 1985, signaled his intention to broaden people-to-people exchanges with the Soviet Union. In his address, he called for exchanges of fraternal, religious, educational and cultural groups.

On educational exchanges, the President, reverting to the American predilection for "thousands," asked why we should not exchange "thousands of undergraduates each year, and even younger students who would live with a host family and attend schools or summer camps?" He also called for increased scholarship programs, courses in history, culture and other subjects, new sister cities, the establishment of libraries and cultural centers (by each country in the other) and an increase in athletic competitions.

The President also asked why, if Soviet spokesmen are free to appear on American television, the Soviet people should not have the same right to see Americans on Soviet television.

Mr. Reagan said he would propose "the broadest people-to-people exchange in the history of the American-Soviet relations, exchanges in sports and culture, in the media, education and the arts" to build "thousands of coalitions for cooperation and peace." He made it clear, however, that these would be private sector programs—at least on the U.S. side—and that governments should "step out of the way . . . once they get the ball rolling."[6]

The Joint Statement, issued on November 21 by the two governments at the conclusion of the Geneva summit, states that President Reagan and General Secretary Gorbachev ". . . believe that there should be greater understanding among our peoples and that to this end they will encourage greater travel and people-to-people contact." Under the heading "Exchange Initiatives," the Joint Statement lists six initiatives:

> The two leaders agreed on the utility of broadening exchanges and contacts including some of their new forms in a number of scientific, educational, medical and sports fields (inter alia, cooperation in the development of educational exchanges and software for elementary and secondary school instruction; measures to promote Russian language studies in the United States and English language studies in the USSR; the annual exchange of professors to conduct special courses in history, culture and economics at the relevant departments of Soviet and American institutions of higher education; mutual allocation of scholarships for the best students in the natural sciences, technology, social sciences and humanities for the period of an academic year; holding regular meets in various sports and increased television coverage of sports events). The two sides agreed to resume cooperation in combatting cancer diseases. The relevant agencies in each of the countries are being instructed to develop specific programs for these exchanges. The resulting programs will be reviewed by the leaders at their next meeting.[7]

The Geneva White House announced later that day that "once the two governments had opened the doors to this kind of exchange, the Administration will look to the people to take the lead." The President, it concluded, will appoint a high-ranking administration official to work with the private sector to ensure the realization of these initiatives, and the resulting programs will be reviewed by the two leaders at their next meeting.[8]

U.S. officials have made it clear that the six initiatives are meant to be illustrative, and not inclusive. The United States, for example, one month before the summit, presented twenty-five exchange proposals to the Soviets who, in turn, proposed twelve of their own. At Geneva, after agreement was reached on the six initiatives, it was also agreed that no areas of exchanges would be closed to future discussion.

A closer examination of the six initiatives, which the White House press release described as new, will show that most of them are not really new but have their origins in the 1970s, the détente years of the Nixon administration.

The annual exchange of professors to lecture in universities of the two countries, under the Fulbright Program, was included in the 1972 cultural agreement. The actual exchange began in 1974 when seven

American and four Soviet professors were exchanged, and it has continued each year.

A scholarship program for the "best students" of the two countries is new if it applies to undergraduates, which the Soviets reportedly have agreed to "in principle," although they have indicated that they want their undergraduates to study at U.S. universities in groups of five and to be accompanied by an "administrative" person.

"Measures to promote" the study of Russian in the United States was included in the Joint U.S.-Soviet Communiqué of May 29, 1972, at the 1972 Nixon-Brezhnev summit, and was also mentioned in the next Program of Exchanges for 1974–1976. There was no mention of the study of English in the Soviet Union in those years because the Soviets were already conducting an extensive English-teaching program in their schools and universities.

Joint programs of cancer research have been conducted by the two governments since 1972 under the Agreement on Cooperation in the Field of Medical Science and Public Health, signed at the 1972 Nixon-Brezhnev summit.

Cooperation in the development of computer software for education is new, but it has been on the Soviet shopping list for exchanges with the United States since the mid-1970s when two Soviet delegations in this field visited the United States under the cultural agreement.

An expansion of sports contacts may be new, as well as increased television coverage of sports events, but sports competitions between the two countries have been held regularly since the early years of the cultural agreement. These exchanges, and their television coverage, expanded greatly during the détente years, and it is difficult to see what more can be done in this area except more of the same.

Despite endorsement of the six initiatives at the highest level, the administration has made it clear that activities under the new initiatives are to be funded, not by the U.S. government, but by the private sector.

This was emphasized by USIA Director Charles Z. Wick at a meeting he called on December 12, 1985, for representatives of private sector organizations involved in Soviet-American exchanges. Wick said that the U.S. government would act as a go-between to help arrange new exchanges with the Soviets, but there would be no U.S. government funding for them.

To encourage and coordinate U.S. efforts under the six initiatives, a Coordinator's Office was established in USIA in January 1986, headed by Dr. Stephen H. Rhinesmith. Rhinesmith is a former president of the American Field Service which conducts a number of international exchange programs.

Without some U.S. government funding it is difficult to see how the exchanges under the six initiatives can take place on the scale foreseen by the administration. Athletic competitions are self-funded. But exchanges of students and university lecturers, and measures to promote the study of Russian in the United States are very expensive, and it is questionable whether they can take place on a large scale without some government seed money. And the Soviets are certainly not prepared for large-scale exchanges of students at the undergraduate level. The "thousands of students" envisioned by many prominent Americans is still very far in the future of Soviet-American exchanges.

The administration expects to obtain private funding for exchanges under the six initiatives, and it may succeed initially. But if these exchanges are to continue over the long run, as they should in order to achieve lasting results, the funding must be there year after year.

Predicting the future course of Soviet-American exchanges is always risky because they are subject to the vagaries of bilateral relations. But it is likely that the initial euphoria of the exchanges agreed to at the Reagan-Gorbachev 1985 summit will not be much different from the euphoria of those which began at the Nixon-Brezhnev summits of the early 1970s.

The U.S. governmental and private sector organizations that enthusiastically began exchanges with the Soviets in the early 1970s soon came up against the harsh realities of trying to cooperate with a closed society, the high costs of the exchanges, the lack of mutual benefit in some cases and the unforeseen political events which intervened.

Exchanges will increase between the two countries, but the pace cannot be faster than the Soviets are willing to accept. Indeed, perhaps the greatest obstacle to a major expansion in exchanges is the inability of the Soviet system to absorb them. The pace will have to be set by the Soviets.

Notes

1. *Weekly Compilation of Presidential Documents* 20, no. 26 (Washington, D.C.: Office of the Federal Register, National Archives and Records Administration), pp. 944–946.

2. *New York Times*, November 27, 1985, p. A14.

3. The full text of the 1985 cultural agreement may be found in Appendix B. For the text of the 1973 agreement, see *United States Treaties and Other International Agreements* 7649, vol. 24, pt. 2, 1973, pp. 1395–1438.

4. The text of the "Annex to the Program of Cooperation and Exchanges" is not appended to this study. Copies may be obtained from the United States Information Agency, Washington, D.C. 20547.

5. Robert F. Byrnes, in *Perspectives: Relations Between the United States and the Soviet Union* (Washington, D.C.: U.S. Government Printing Office, 1979), pp. 422–426.

6. *Weekly Compilation of Presidential Documents* 21, no. 46, pp. 1399–1402.

7. *Weekly Compilation of Presidential Documents* 21, no. 47, pp. 1422–1424.

8. Press Release, November 21, 1985, The White House, Office of the Press Secretary, Geneva, Switzerland.

12

Eastern Europe

Introduction

Any study of U.S.-Soviet exchanges should also consider U.S. exchanges with Eastern Europe because the two are related. What happens in the Soviet Union affects Eastern Europe, for they are bound together politically, economically and militarily, if not culturally. But what happens in Eastern Europe also affects the Soviet Union.

Eastern Europe, for this study, comprises Poland, Yugoslavia, Romania, Bulgaria, Hungary, Czechoslovakia and East Germany, in the order they will be discussed. The Yugoslavs object strenuously to being included in Eastern Europe because they are not a member of the Warsaw Pact but rather the "neutral and nonaligned" group of states. However, in U.S. government and many private sector exchanges they are usually grouped with the East Europeans. Albania is not included because there have been no U.S. exchanges with that remote and withdrawn country.

Each of these countries is different from the others, some of them very different, and their cultural exchanges with the United States, as a consequence, have also been different.

Most of the region, throughout much of its past, has been a part of Europe in its culture and, until recently, in its economics and politics as well. But since the end of World War II, with Yugoslavia excepted, Eastern Europe has been a part of the Soviet empire. Its cultural ties with the West have endured, nevertheless. These ties were interrupted during World War II and the immediate postwar years, but when the opportunity came, each country sought to reestablish its cultural ties with Europe and the United States, at its own pace and in its own way.

Poland

The "Polish October" revolution in 1956 ended the rule of a Stalinist regime and brought to power a national communist government that, while remaining allied with the Soviet Union and following it completely in international affairs, demonstrated a surprising degree of independence in its domestic affairs. The forced collectivization of agriculture ended and the private ownership of farms was accepted. The Roman Catholic Church, a symbol of Polish nationalism, was given considerable freedom.   And Poland's traditional cultural channels to the West were reopened.

The Ford and Rockefeller Foundations were the first to take advantage of this breach in the hitherto impregnable Iron Curtain. The two foundations, in 1957, began fellowship programs in Poland— Ford, in the social sciences and humanities, and Rockefeller, in agriculture and the biological sciences—that were to bring hundreds of Polish scholars and scientists to Western Europe and the United States for study and research.   The Polish government welcomed these initiatives.   Passport and exit visa policies for Polish citizens were liberal, and other American foundations soon followed.

The U.S. government also responded to the Polish government's receptivity to exchanges with the West. Under the Fulbright Program, introduced in 1960, Polish and American students were exchanged, and U.S. professors lectured in American studies at Polish universities in exchange for Polish scholars who did research at U.S. universities. The American Embassy conducted an active cultural program, without objection by the Polish government. A library was opened in the American Embassy in Warsaw to which the Polish authorities permitted access by the public. The State Department's International Visitor Program brought Polish leaders to the United States for visits of up to four weeks. An exchange of U.S. and Polish performing artists began.   And with the Polish currency that accrued to the U.S. government from the sale to Poland of surplus U.S. agricultural commodities, joint research by Polish and U.S. scientists began in a number of fields of common interest to the two countries.

A lively exchange began in many scientific and scholarly fields, and soon hundreds of Poles were conducting research in the United States each year on the invitation of U.S. universities and research institutions.   These contacts led to the establishment of direct exchanges between Polish and U.S. universities, and by the mid-1970s there were more than twenty such arrangements.   When the Ford Foundation in 1968 finally ended its Polish fellowship program—because the Polish government refused to give it a free hand in selecting applicants—Ford's place was taken by IREX which began a reciprocal scholarly exchange with Poland, funded by Ford.

These exchanges flourished without a cultural agreement between the two governments. In the 1970s, however, the Polish government several times proposed a cultural agreement, in an effort to reestablish its control over what had become literally a free market in cultural exchanges with the West. Through an agreement, it also sought to exact a degree of reciprocity for Polish cultural and information programs in the United States in exchange for what it was permitting the United States to do in Poland. The U.S. response to these proposals for a cultural agreement was always a polite "No," which the Polish government reluctantly accepted because it realized that it was the "most favored nation" in U.S. exchanges with Eastern Europe.

The Department of State and USIA were pleased with their ability to conduct exchanges and cultural programs in Poland without the strictures of an intergovernmental agreement, and they often cited Poland as an example of how they would like to conduct exchanges with other communist countries.

Much of this activity came to a halt in December 1981 when martial law was declared and strict travel controls were imposed by the Polish military regime. Much of the American Embassy's cultural program was curtailed by the Polish authorities. Academic exchanges continued, however, including the Fulbright and IREX exchanges. Performing arts exchanges also continued, on a commercial basis without U.S. government involvement. That these activities were not curtailed is evidence of how much they are valued by both sides.

If Washington's political problems with Warsaw can be resolved in the wake of improved U.S.-USSR relations, U.S. exchanges with Poland will return to their previous level. Poland is the largest and most important country in Eastern Europe. The United States has had an historic relationship with Poland, and it is no exaggeration to say that the United States enjoys more popular support in Poland than in any other European country. And there are some eight million Americans of Polish origin who support these exchanges.

Yugoslavia

Yugoslavia broke with Moscow in 1948, but it was not until ten years later that exchanges with the United States began, with Ford Foundation fellowships, as in the case of Poland. And, like Poland, a liberal Yugoslav policy on passports and visas soon encouraged other U.S. foundations and universities, as well as the State Department, to begin exchange programs there. As elsewhere in Eastern Europe, the Ford program was succeeded by IREX in 1968.

Yugoslavia has permitted USIA to maintain field posts and cultural centers in Belgrade and provincial cities, the only communist country in Europe to do so.

In Yugoslavia there was also local currency which had accrued to the U.S. government from the sale of surplus agricultural commodities. These funds were used to pay some of the costs of the exchange programs, both governmental and private, as well as cooperative scientific research between the two governments.

Under a U.S. policy of normalizing relations with Yugoslavia, a "Fulbright" Binational Commission was established in 1964 to administer educational exchanges between the two countries under the Fulbright Program. Yugoslavia thus became the first, and only, communist country to have such a commission. By 1986 the Yugoslav Fulbright Program had become the second largest in Europe, second only to the one in the Federal Republic of Germany.

The Commission, comprised of citizens of the two countries appointed by their governments, sets policy for academic exchanges which are funded jointly by the two governments and administers them through a staff in Belgrade headed by a Yugoslav citizen.

Yugoslavia, like Poland, has also sought a cultural agreement with the United States at various times, but the U.S. government has demurred. In 1981, however, in response to Yugoslav requests for more formal cultural consultations between the two governments, the United States agreed to the establishment of a U.S.-Yugoslav Joint Cultural Working Group. The Group meets each year, alternatively in the United States and Yugoslavia, to review cultural activities between the two countries.

In cultural exchanges, Yugoslavia has been treated by the United States as a West rather than an East European country. But what distinguishes Yugoslav exchanges from those with other European countries, both West and East, is not so much its communist government, but the makeup of its federal system, six republics and two autonomous regions, and their relationship to the federal government. Figuring out how this works—or does not work—is half the job of conducting exchanges with Yugoslavia.

Romania

In 1960, two years after signature of the first U.S.-USSR cultural agreement, Romania made its move to establish cultural exchanges with the United States and, like the Soviets, it chose to do so through an intergovernmental agreement.

Romania is considered a maverick in the Warsaw Pact, and there are good reasons for this. A non-Slavic people surrounded by Slavs on three sides and by Hungarians on the other, and buffeted by wars and territorial disputes with its neighbors at various times in their history, Romanians have always sought, above all, to maintain their national independence and cultural identity.

Unlike Poland and Yugoslavia, a cultural agreement with the United States was a firm requirement, reflecting the Romanian preference for conducting exchanges on a government-to-government basis, and its insistence on maintaining complete control over its cultural relations with other countries. The Ford Foundation program in Romania, for example, did not begin until 1965, after the Romanians had several years of experience in exchanges with the West.

Romania's main interests in exchanges with the United States were in obtaining grants for its scientists, engineers and scholars to study abroad, and in sending professors to lecture in Romanian studies at U.S. universities. In exchange, it was willing to accept American students as well as university lecturers in English teaching and American studies. The American Embassy in Bucharest was also permitted to conduct a modest cultural and information program.

U.S. exchanges with Romania reached their peak during the mid-1970s when Romanian and U.S. government policies both called for increased exchanges. Each successive two-year cultural agreement provided for increased numbers of Romanians to visit and study in the United States and equal numbers of Americans to do the same in Romania. The Romanian objective was to train more scientists and engineers in areas important to Romania's economic development. The U.S. objective was to strengthen bilateral relations and to reward Romania for its sometimes independent stance from the Soviet Union.

The exchange circuits, however, were soon overloaded and the fuse blew. Romanian exchange visitors began to defect to the West in increasing numbers, seeking to escape an authoritarian and oppressive regime at home and to improve their economic status abroad. With each defection the Romanians tightened up their screening procedures for travel abroad and, as a result, the pool of those eligible to travel diminished rapidly.

It also became difficult for the United States to recruit qualified Americans to go to Romania. Living conditions there were harsh, and the local population was discouraged by the security police from being friendly with foreigners. And there were more pleasant places in Eastern Europe for an American to go on exchange.

As a consequence, the U.S.-Romanian program was cut back in the late 1970s, and U.S. government funds that formerly had been allocated to Romanian exchanges were transferred to other countries in Eastern Europe where the conditions for exchanges were more favorable.

One bright light for U.S. government cultural programs was the establishment of an American Library in Bucharest—actually a cultural center—outside Embassy premises and open to the Romanian public. The opening of American libraries in communist countries, accessible to the public, has long been a USIA priority, and the opportunity in Romania came when President Nixon visited there in 1969. The Romanians readily agreed to permit an American Library in Bucharest in exchange for a Romanian library in New York City. The two libraries still exist today.

Bulgaria

When the Helsinki Accords were signed in 1975, they endorsed exchange agreements between signatory states and accordingly gave the green light to Hungary, Czechoslovakia and Bulgaria—countries which for various reasons had limited their exchanges with the United States—to open negotiations with the United States on general agreements in culture, education, science and technology.

Negotiations opened with all three countries at about the same time, and it was thought at the State Department that they would be wrapped up in the following order—Hungary, Czechoslavakia and Bulgaria.

Hungary, the most liberal East European country after Poland at that time, was expected to present few problems in reaching agreement. Czechoslavakia would be next, it was thought, because of its high interest in science and technology exchanges. Bulgaria was expected to be last because of its tight domestic politics and its close dependency on the Soviet Union.

The Bulgarians, however, turned out to be most eager to sign an exchange agreement with the United States. There had been a small IUCTG scholar exchange since 1963—succeeded by IREX in 1968—and an exchange of one or two university lecturers each year under the Fulbright program. The Bulgars, however, wanted to obtain more grants for their scientists and scholars to study in the United States and to send lecturers in Bulgarian studies to teach at U.S. universities. They therefore presented few difficulties in negotiating a general agreement on exchanges which was signed in 1977.

With the agreement signed, a modest program began and has continued without interruption. The number of exchanges in all fields covered by the agreement, however, has not been large because of limited funding provided by the U.S. government—due to the relatively low priority given Bulgaria in Eastern Europe—and by limited interest in Bulgaria on the part of U.S. academia and the general public.

But the interest and desire are there on the part of the Bulgarian government which sees scientific and cultural exchanges—in that order—as important for a developing country. Through scientific exchanges it can acquire training and technology easily, quickly and cheaply. Through cultural exchanges it can establish a cultural presence abroad for a small and relatively little known European country.

Hungary

Hungary should have been an active exchange partner of the United States in the late 1950s. A thoroughly Western country with a strong national culture, an advanced industrial, scientific and scholarly base and a tradition of excellence in these fields as well as the arts, Hungary should have joined Poland, Romania and Yugoslavia in expanding cultural exchanges with the United States in the late 1950s.

But Hungary, in 1956, had gone through a national revolution which had been brutally suppressed by the Soviet Union. Neither Budapest nor Washington found the 1950s and 1960s the right time for cultural exchanges. Cultural activities of the American Embassy were severely circumscribed, and the Hungarians were not inclined to conduct exchanges with the U.S. government.

The Hungarians were willing, nevertheless, to work with the U.S. private sector. A small reciprocal exchange of scholars was begun with IUCTG in 1963—to be succeeded by IREX in 1968—and a Ford Foundation fellowship program was begun in 1962.

U.S.-Hungarian relations began to improve in the 1970s. A consular convention and a claims settlement were signed in 1972. Secretary of State William P. Rogers visited Budapest in 1973, a Joint Economic Council was established in 1975, the final debts between the two governments were paid in 1976 and a general agreement on culture, education, science and technology was concluded in 1977.

There remained, however, a program of exchanges to be negotiated under the general agreement, and that had to await resolution of yet one more issue in bilateral relations, the return of the Hungarian crown.

The Hungarian crown of Saint Stephen, Hungary's first Catholic king and its patron saint, has been a symbol of national pride and legitimacy throughout Hungary's history. The crown had come into the possession of the U.S. Army in the closing months of World War II, and it was being held by the United States pending its return to a legitimate Hungarian government. It took time before Hungarian emigres abroad, and in turn the U.S. government, were to become reconciled to returning the crown to a communist government in Budapest, and that is what finally happened in 1978, assisted by the American Ambassador to Hungary, Philip M. Kaiser.

With the crown safely home in Budapest, negotiations proceeded for the program of exchanges—the details of exactly what would be exchanged under the general agreement—and this is where another hangup occurred.

The Hungarians were cautious on two counts. First, they feared that under a general agreement, culture and education would be given priority over science and technology. The Hungarian authorities had wanted a separate agreement on science and technology, along the lines of the U.S.-USSR Science and Technology Agreement, but the U.S. negotiators had held out for a general agreement. Failing to get a separate science agreement, Hungary then sought a separate program for science annexed to the general agreement. Second, the Hungarians feared that, as a small country, they would be overwhelmed by a large cultural and information program conducted by USIA.

As a consequence, the Hungarians held out, during the negotiations, for getting as much science and technology into the program of exchanges before agreeing to the culture and information.

As a further complication, the negotiations on the Hungarian side were conducted by the Hungarian Cultural Institute—known by its Hungarian initials KKI—a strange amalgam of interests in foreign relations, culture, science and—last but not least—intelligence, and somewhat analogous to the long defunct USSR State Committee for Cultural Relations with Foreign Countries. In its negotiating tactics, the KKI combined the most salient features of the Hungarian communist and Austro-Hungarian bureaucracies, and in its administration of exchanges it was often as much an impediment as a facilitator. The KKI was eventually phased out in the early 1980s, and its exchange responsibilities were distributed among various other government agencies.

After the program of exchanges was finally signed in 1979, U.S.-Hungary exchanges experienced a slow but steady growth, assisted by a liberalizing trend in Hungarian domestic politics and improved bilateral relations. The program has been renewed several times for two-year periods since 1979, without major difficulties.

Hungarians coming to the United States under the exchange program generally have been very well qualified in their fields. In turn, Americans travelling to Hungary have found it a very pleasant country to visit. And Hungarian science, among the best in Europe in many fields, has benefitted from the exchange, its fears of losing out to culture and education having proven groundless.

Czechoslovakia

Czechoslovakia in the mid-1970s would have been an easy country to negotiate a cutural agreement with, but several events intervened.

Another thoroughly Western country in its history and culture—Prague was once the seat of the Holy Roman Empire, and it is geographically farther west than Vienna—Czechoslovakia, in the late 1950s, did not follow the lead of its Polish neighbor in restoring cultural contacts with the West. In fact, the Polish October and its reopening of contacts with the West caused an already hardline Czechoslovak regime to be even more wary of relaxing its internal grip.

Like Bulgaria and Hungary, Czechoslovakia initially eschewed exchanges with the U.S. government, but it readily agreed to a scholar exchange with IUCTG in 1963 and a Ford Foundation fellowship program in 1968. The motivation, as elsewhere in Eastern Europe, was access to U.S. science and technology. During the 1960s, Czechoslovakia also allowed increasing numbers of its scientists and scholars to accept invitations from U.S. institutions to conduct research in the United States. Indeed, when the Soviets invaded Czechoslovakia in 1968, there were as many as 422 Czechoslovaks in the United States on research grants.[1]

The Soviet invasion and the end of the Prague Spring, the movement for internal reform, severely limited exchanges with the United States. Passport controls were tightened and it became very difficult for Czechoslovak citizens to travel abroad.

With détente, efforts to improve U.S.-Czechoslovak bilateral relations began. A consular convention was signed in 1973—although it was not ratified until 1980. And with the signature of the Helsinki Accords in 1975, the way seemed clear for a general agreement on exchanges. Czechoslovakia, however, proved to be even more difficult than Hungary in negotiating an agreement.

The main stumbling block was the Czechoslovak request for a separate science and technology agreement, similar to that which the United States had signed with the Soviet Union. The Czechoslovak government did not want its science and technology exchanges to be part of a general agreement which included culture and education. Unlike the situation in Hungary, the negotiations ended in an impasse in 1977 when Czechoslovakia refused to accept a general agreement comprising culture, education, science and technology.

It took another nine years before the cautious Prague government overcame its hesitation and signed a general agreement on exchanges in April 1986, only four months after the Soviets signed their new cultural agreement with the United States at Geneva. The Czechoslovak authorities thus demonstrated again that it is always easier for them to follow the Soviet lead.

East Germany

Until the mid-1970s, it was "the German problem," the reluctance of the United States and other NATO powers to establish diplomatic relations with East Germany and thereby contravene the non-recognition policy of their West German ally, the Federal Republic of Germany. In the absence of diplomatic relations, there was no possibility for the governments of the United States and East Germany to initiate cultural, educational or scientific exchanges.

The East Germans had high interest in exchanges with the United States, but any progress in this area had to await the establishment of diplomatic relations. After diplomatic recognition came in 1974, the German Democratic Republic began an exchange of scholars with IREX in 1975, and permitted its universities to enter into direct exchanges with U.S. universities. It also permitted the American Embassy in East Berlin to conduct a modest cultural program.

Informal talks between the two governments on a cultural agreement, held in 1978 and 1979, were without result. The State Department wanted to normalize relations, but there were other issues of higher priority to be resolved before a cultural agreement could be signed. And the East Germans, in these talks, refused to guarantee the right of access by their citizens to the modest library in the American Embassy in East Berlin, which was a USIA requirement for an agreement.

Subsequent political events also intervened. The Soviet invasion of Afghanistan, the rise of the Solidarity movement in neighboring Poland, the imposition of martial law in Poland and the resultant cooling in relations with the United States all served to put off the negotiation of a cultural agreement. And in 1986, there were further differences with East Germany over the status of Berlin and the Libyan terrorism connection. As a consequence, in mid-1986 there was no cultural agreement in sight, and the U.S. government seemed to be in no hurry to conclude one.

Conclusion

The Reagan-Gorbachev Geneva summit, as with the Nixon-Brezhnev summits, has once again put the spotlight on Soviet-American relations, and the U.S. government and private sector in 1986 are gearing up for an expanded program of exchanges with the Soviet Union. In the process, U.S. exchanges with Eastern Europe are likely to suffer, particularly in a period of budgetary restraint.

In strategic terms, the Soviet Union is more important to the United States than Eastern Europe. But it would be shortsighted for the United States to cut back its exchanges with Eastern Europe in favor of those with the Soviet Union. Eastern Europe, in the past, has been Russia's window to the West, and this has not changed today. In our time, sociology came to the Soviet Union via Poland and Yugoslavia as a consequence of the training which sociologists of those countries received through Ford Foundation fellowships. Hungary in the mid-1980s is providing for the Soviet Union useful examples in economic reforms. Soviet citizens travel more freely to Eastern Europe than to the West, and it is through Eastern Europe that they get their ideas from the West. In fact, Warsaw, Prague, Berlin and Budapest are the West for Soviet citizens today.

Through exchanges, the United States can accomplish much in Eastern Europe that will help to realize its objectives in the Soviet Union, but without the hassle and at much less cost.

Notes

1. "Survey of U.S. Educational and Cultural Exchanges with the Soviet Union and Eastern Europe," a classified report prepared by Boris H. Klosson for the Department of State on June 23, 1978, and declassified and released under the Freedom of Information Act on December 24, 1984, p. 73.

13

Recommendations

Cultural exchanges play a modest role in Soviet-American relations, but one whose importance has been recognized by both countries for its long-range benefits.

But if exchanges are to be effective over the long run, they must be insulated from the ups and downs in bilateral relations. Exchanges can be most useful, and even necessary, when relations are strained and sustained dialogue is required.

When negotiations to renew the cultural agreement were recessed in mid-December 1979, it was expected that they would resume early in 1980. The negotiations, however, became hostage to unforeseen events—the Soviet invasion of Afghanistan, martial law in Poland, the Korean Airline shootdown and the resultant deterioration in bilateral relations.

Reducing the U.S. government role in exchanges will help to ensure that they will continue in bad times as well as good, with or without an intergovernmental agreement. As we have seen, many private sector exchanges in culture and education continued for six years without an agreement. The private sector in the United States is predominant in most of the fields covered by the agreement, and the private sector should play the lead role.

Private sector programs are easier to negotiate and administer than governmental programs, as well as less costly. In negotiations between governments, minor issues are often magnified and lead to confrontations in which each side is unwilling to back down. Where the U.S. government wishes to initiate an exchange or to support an existing one, it can easily do so by making a grant to a private sector institution interested in conducting the exchange. A mix of private sector and governmental programs has characterized U.S.-USSR exchanges since their inception, and the trend over the years has been to transfer more of the activity to the private sector. This will continue, particularly if President Reagan's U.S.-Soviet Exchange Initiative proves to be successful.

But is the intergovernmental agreement really needed if the private sector plays the lead role? Educational and scholarly exchanges continued between 1980 and 1985 without the agreement. Soviet artists can perform in the United States without the agreement, as seen by the performance of pianist Emil Gilels in New York in April 1983. And it is likely that the Soviets would have accepted American artists if the administration had indicated that it wished to resume performing arts exchanges, and if the political climate had been right. Museum exchanges require only a U.S. government determination that they are in the national interest. Sports, tourism and even the exchange of the government-published magazines, *Amerika* and *Soviet Life*, continued without the agreement. Only USIA's thematic exhibitions require the cultural agreement, since the Soviets will not accept them unless required to do so as part of a package deal under the agreement.

A reduced role for government in Soviet-American exchanges—and its eventual elimination—has been advocated by Robert F. Byrnes, Distinguished Professor of History at Indiana University.[1] Byrnes was a founder of the Inter-University Committee on Travel Grants in 1956, and served as its chairman from 1960 to 1968, during which time he represented the United States in scholarly exchanges with the Soviet Union and Eastern Europe.

Byrnes argues that exchanges have given the United States some influence within the Soviet system, but the concomitant government involvement in U.S. intellectual life makes Washington resemble, in his words, "St. Petersburg on the Potomac." He is critical of Washington for acquiescing to Soviet restrictions on access and travel by Americans in the Soviet Union and for tolerating these restrictions for more than twenty-five years. He also believes there is a moral cost in exchanging scholars with a country which restrains and imprisons its intellectuals.

We should phase out formal exchange agreements, Byrnes says, which involve private sector institutions and set quotas for persons to be exchanged as if they were sacks of grain. In 1979, he proposed that the quota system for exchanges should be ended by 1984—a symbolic year—and that the United States should press instead for a free flow of persons, books and other cultural materials. Byrnes recommends not restricting Soviet scholars in the United States, but granting them access to our resources only as the Soviet Union progressively moves toward relaxing its controls. And private institutions, he concludes, should establish a loose federation to maintain an overview of exchanges and to set policy to ensure opportunities for Americans in the Soviet Union equal to those which the Soviets enjoy in the United States.

Byrnes' views are a desirable standard for the long term, but in the near term they raise the prospect of forgoing exchanges until the Soviet system changes, which will be a long time coming. In the near term, it can be argued, it is precisely the mix of government and private sector activities that requires a cultural agreement. The private sector and the government have a mutual interest in Soviet exchanges and in ensuring their success to the extent possible. The differences between an open and a closed society are at their starkest in cultural exchanges, and there will be a continuing need for some government role to protect U.S. interests as a whole.

An intergovernmental agreement provides this protection by giving the blessings of both governments to the various exchanges it encompasses, and by providing a mechanism to monitor reciprocity, equality and mutuality of benefits. An agreement also provides for periodic consultations between the governments to assess the progress of exchanges and to renegotiate the agreement.

The actual exchanges, their content and how they are conducted, should be left to the participating organizations on both sides.

It may be argued that this would fragment the U.S. effort in exchanges and would pit U.S. private sector organizations against a unified and coordinated Soviet exchange effort to the detriment of overall U.S. interests.

This argument overlooks the evidence that some Soviet ministries and agencies have a greater interest in exchanges than others and, depending on how much clout they may have within the Soviet system, are consequently easier to negotiate with. I have personally witnessed arguments between Soviet ministry officials and organizations under their jurisdiction about who will negotiate with the Americans, and how. It is not in the U.S. interest to oppose whatever small stirrings of pluralism there may be in Soviet society. The United States should not become highly centralized like the Soviet Union in order to deal with it on cultural exchanges.

To be sure, not all U.S. private sector organizations have the experience and negotiating skills to deal directly with the Soviets. Some of them tend, initially, to be too ready to accede to Soviet demands without getting anything in return, and they are often bested by the Soviets in the first round of exchanges. But most Americans soon learn how to deal with the Soviets and, in the process, the country as a whole gains.

The U.S. government alone does not have the resources to conduct cultural exchanges with the Soviet Union, and for this it needs private sector participation. An intergovernmental agreement which includes a mix of government and private sector activities provides the United States with the leverage it needs should the Soviet Union abuse U.S. hospitality or fail to provide similar exchange opportunities for Americans in the Soviet Union.

But how, it may be asked, does the United States obtain reciprocity for the visits by Georgy Arbatov and other Soviet spokesmen who accept all-expenses-paid invitations from U.S. organizations which provide a platform for promoting Soviet policies before American audiences, or for Soviet columnists who are published by U.S. newspapers while Soviet newspapers are closed to U.S. writers?

U.S. organizations which invite Soviets to the United States can request reciprocity, if they wish, and send their representatives to the Soviet Union at Soviet cost. Conditions for exchanges will never be the same in the two countries, but the Soviets are prepared to provide reciprocity if it is requested. In this respect, the new cultural agreement signed in November 1985 does provide for appearances by representatives of each country on the television of the other.[2] Further progress toward equal exposure in the media of the two countries would be a worthy goal in the negotiation of future cultural agreements.

And if the U.S., government or private organization chooses not to request reciprocity, the United States, as the stronger and more self-confident power, can easily afford to permit Soviet access to the American public. We should have nothing to fear from free speech, even from our principal adversary.

Coordination, Monitoring and Assessment

The U.S. government role in coordinating and monitoring educational and cultural exchanges with the Soviet Union and Eastern Europe was found faulty in a report prepared for the Department of State in 1978 by Boris H. Klosson. Mr. Klosson, a career Foreign Service officer, has served as Director of the Department's Soviet and Eastern European Exchanges Staff in the 1960s and as Deputy Chief of Mission in Moscow in the 1970s.[3]

The Klosson report found that, as exchanges have expanded, the U.S. government capacity to monitor them has become diluted and dispersed. Among the report's major findings were: the increased demands of day-to-day operations prevent officials from having a complete picture of what is going on and how much is being spent (in Fiscal Year 1977, the report said, the U.S. government was expending an estimated ten million dollars, exclusive of staff costs, for educational and cultural exchanges with the Soviet Union and Eastern Europe), evaluation of U.S. past experience is inadequate and there is no overall assessment of how the United States has benefited, the impact abroad is largely undocumented, it is uncertain where the United States wants to proceed in exchanges with the Soviet Union and Eastern Europe, there is no clear statement of objectives, individual agencies set their own goals and there is no mechanism for review in terms of an integrated government-wide program.

Klosson recommended giving State the responsibility for coordination, review and planning through the Interagency Coordinating Committee for U.S.-Soviet Affairs (ICCUSA), which is chaired by State, and that an up-to-date statement of U.S. policy on exchanges be prepared.

Eight years later, in 1986, the situation described in the Klosson report had not changed appreciably. At State, the staff for monitoring exchanges with the Soviet Union was down to one officer and a few support personnel. At USIA, there was no central point for monitoring and assessing these exchanges, and responsibility was divided between the new office for the Presidential Initiative and various other elements of the Agency. Monitoring of exchanges by ICCUSA was said to be on an ad-hoc basis. There were several policy papers on various aspects of exchanges, but no overall up-to-date paper.

Exchanges with the Soviet Union had declined, to be sure, between 1980 and 1986, and this reduced the need for monitoring and evaluation. But in 1986, as Soviet-American exchanges appear to be entering another period of growth, these deficiencies need to be remedied.

Who Wins?

Who wins, we or the Russians? The question is misleading because the two sides have different objectives in exchanges. The simple answer, for those who need one, is that we both win. In some exchanges there may be an imbalance in numbers and mutual benefits, and the conditions under which exchanges are conducted in the two countries are certainly not equal. But in all these exchanges there is some benefit to both sides.

The challenge for U.S. government officials who oversee exchanges is to look at the entire program of exchanges between the two countries and to decide how best to balance the benefits.

The existence of these exchanges for twenty-two years under an intergovernmental agreement, their continuation for another six years without an agreement, and their resumption under a new agreement signed at a U.S.-Soviet summit meeting indicate that both sides find them mutually beneficial.

They have been endorsed by seven U.S. administrations from Eisenhower to Reagan. There is broad support in the Congress, which has approved funds for these exchanges year after year, and among U.S. government agencies that have participated in them. And in the final test, there is sufficient evidence that they enjoy the broad support of the U.S. public, particularly in the academic, cultural and scientific communities.

On the Soviet side, there is evidence that the government finds these exchanges useful and wants them to continue. There are, of course, the self-serving interests—to acquire technology, to demonstrate Soviet achievements, to promote Soviet views abroad and to be accepted by the United States as a coequal. But the Soviet authorities are also under pressure from their own scientists, scholars, cultural figures, athletes and others who want to travel abroad, not only for personal reasons—to learn what is going on in their fields of interest—but also because it is in the Russian historic tradition to travel to, and learn from, the West. This should be encouraged.

Skeptics of the value of cultural exchanges with the Soviet Union are advised to look back to the 1950s, before the exchanges with the West began. At that time, the Soviet authorities had a monopoly of information on what was said in their country about the Soviet Union and the rest of the world. Objective knowledge about other countries was practically nonexistent. The Soviet Union, which occupies one-sixth of the world's surface, was a vast unknown to the rest of the world. There was no human rights movement in the Soviet Union, no emigration and no vocal dissident movement. And until 1958 and the start of exchanges, there were only a few Americans who had any direct knowledge of the Soviet Union, our principal adversary.

To ascribe all of the changes in the Soviet Union since 1958 to exchanges with the West would be going too far. It is clear, however, that many of the changes have occurred because the Soviet Union has had increasing contact with the people and ideas of other countries.

One important result of exchanges has been to break the Soviet monopoly on information. This explains why Soviet authorities were so fearful of exchanges when they began, and why they are still apprehensive today about any further loosening of their control of information. Knowledge is power, and exchanges bring knowledge to Soviet citizens about their own country and the outside world.

Exchanges also bring knowledge about the Soviet Union to the United States, enabling it to have a more realistic view of its principal adversary and to more accurately assess its strengths and weaknesses. Exchanges are now a well-established element in U.S.-USSR relations. The major issue today is how they should be conducted for maximum benefit to the United States. In seeking to answer this question, I hope that practitioners of exchanges, as well as those who set policy for them, will find this study useful.

Notes

1. *Perspectives: Relations Between the United States and the Soviet Union* (Washington, D.C.: U.S. Government Printing Office, 1979), pp. 422–426.

2. See Article 7, para. 2 of the General Agreement in Appendix B.

3. "Survey of U.S. Educational and Cultural Exchanges with the Soviet Union and Eastern Europe," a classified report prepared by Boris H. Klosson for the Department of State on June 23, 1978, and declassified and released under the Freedom of Information Act on December 24, 1984.

Appendix A:
NSC 5607, "East-West Exchanges"

NSC 5607

June 29, 1956

NOTE BY THE EXECUTIVE SECRETARY
to the
NATIONAL SECURITY COUNCIL
on
EAST-WEST EXCHANGES

References: A. NSC 5508/1
              B. NSC 5602/1
              C. NSC Action Nos. 1522-g and 1577
              D. Memos for NSC from Executive Secretary, same
                      subject, dated June 6 and 19, 1956

The National Security Council, the Secretary of the Treasury, the Attorney General, the Secretary of Commerce, the Special Assistant to the President for Disarmament, and the Director, Bureau of the Budget, at the 289th Council meeting on June 28, 1956, discussed the draft statement of policy on the subject, submitted as the Department of State position and transmitted by the reference memorandum of June 6; the recommendations thereon by the NSC Planning Board, transmitted by the reference memorandum of June 19; and the views of the Joint Chiefs of Staff as reported by the Chairman, JCS, at the meeting. The Council adopted the statement of policy, subject to the amendments set forth in NSC Action No. 1577-b.

The President has this date approved the above-mentioned statement of policy, as amended and adopted by the Council and enclosed herewith as NSC 5607, and (1) refers it to the Secretary of State for implementation in consultation with the Department of

Justice and other departments, agencies and boards as appropriate; keeping the Departments of Defense and Commerce and, as appropriate, other interested departments, agencies and boards informed in advance of proposed East-West exchanges; and (2) directs the Secretary of State and the Attorney General to continue to cooperate in developing and applying appropriate internal security safeguards with respect to the admission of Soviet and satellite nationals to the United States.

NSC 5607, as approved, supersedes NSC 5508/1.

JAMES S. LAY, JR.
Executive Secretary

cc: The Secretary of the Treasury
The Attorney General
The Secretary of Commerce
The Special Assistant to the President for Disarmament
The Director, Bureau of the Budget
The Chairman, Joint Chiefs of Staff
The Director of Central Intelligence
The Chairman, IIC
The Chairman, ICIS

STATEMENT OF POLICY
by the
NATIONAL SECURITY COUNCIL
on
EAST-WEST EXCHANGES

GENERAL CONSIDERATIONS

1. The basic strategy of the United States *vis-a-vis* the Soviet bloc is:

a. To promote within Soviet Russia evolution toward a regime which will abandon predatory policies, which will seek to promote the aspirations of the Russian people rather than the global ambitions of International Communism, and which will increasingly rest upon the consent of the governed rather than upon despotic police power.

b. As regards the European satellites, we seek their evolution toward independence of Moscow.

2. For the first time since the end of World War II there are visible signs of progress along the lines we desire.

3. Within the Soviet Union there is increasing education and consequent demand for greater freedom of thought and expression; there is increasing demand for greater personal security than existed under Stalin's police state, and there is increasing demand for more consumer's [sic] goods and better living conditions for the masses of people. The demands referred to must be considerable because the Soviet rulers judge it necessary to take drastic and hazardous measures to seem to meet them.

4. Within the satellite countries there has occurred a considerable demotion of those who were dedicated to the Stalin doctrine of iron discipline of Communists everywhere, with the Soviet Communist Party acting as the general staff of the world proletariat. The fact that "Titoism" is now regarded as respectable by the Soviet rulers, and that it is profitable to Tito, encourages those within the satellite countries such as Czechoslovakia, Poland and Hungary, to seek a greater degree of nationalism and independence of Moscow.

5. There has thus come about a condition which should lead the United States intensively to seek projects which would have impact within the Soviet bloc and encourage the liberal tendencies referred to.

6. At the Geneva meeting of Foreign Ministers, the three Western Powers submitted a well-rounded 17-point proposal which reflected the above thinking. This was rejected by the Soviet Union, which, however, indicated that it might be prepared to develop East-West exchanges along the indicated lines on the basis of bilateral talks.

7. The problem of East-West exchanges should be considered in the foregoing context.

POLICY CONCLUSIONS

8. Our foreign policies are necessarily <u>defensive</u>, so far as the use of force is concerned. But they can be <u>offensive</u> in terms of promoting a desire for greater individual freedom, well-being and security within the Soviet Union, and greater independence within the satellites. In other words, East-West exchanges should be an implementation of positive United States foreign policy.

9. The exchanges should in large part be initiated by the United States itself, and we should not be content with the negative or neutral position incident to passing upon Soviet initiatives, or the initiatives of private groups within the United States. Of course, Soviet initiatives should be accepted, and the private U.S. initiatives should be welcomed, whenever they advance U.S. policy or seem to be an acceptable and necessary price for what will advance U.S. policy. But the Government should be thinking and planning imaginatively in this field.

10. One aspect of this matter which requires particular consideration is the impact of what we do upon third countries as well as upon military, political and economic cooperation among the countries of the free world. In many cases, the United States can tolerate a type of exchange which to other countries would be poisonous. Consideration should be given to explaining to third countries, on a confidential basis, the scope and purpose of our program and the precautions we would take, so that they will not misconstrue what we do as evidence that we believe that Soviet purposes have now become benign. This could be done, for example, as regards the American Republics at a meeting of the Ambassadors, such as we have had with increasing frequency in recent months. There could be similar expositions made on a selective basis with friendly countries of Africa and Asia. In this way, it could be made clear that what we do is a part of <u>our</u> policy designed to weaken International Communism, and that it is not either an acquiescence in Soviet policy or a recognition that Soviet motives have so changed that they are no longer to be feared.

OBJECTIVES

11. To increase the knowledge of the Soviet and satellite people as to the outer world so that their judgments will be based upon fact and not upon Communist fiction.

12. To encourage freedom of thought by bringing to the Soviet and satellite peoples challenging ideas and demonstrating to Soviet and satellite intellectuals the scope of intellectual freedom which is encouraged within the United States.

13. To stimulate the demand of Soviet and satellite citizens for greater personal security by bringing home to them the degree of personal security which is afforded by our constitutional and legal systems.

14. To stimulate their desire for more consumer's goods by bringing them to realize how rich are the fruits of free labor and how much they themselves could gain from a government which primarily sought their well-being and not conquest.

15. To stimulate nationalism within the satellite countries by reviving the historic traditions of these peoples and by suggesting the great benefits which can be derived from a courageous policy of defiance of Moscow such as Tito exhibited.

COURSES OF ACTION

16. The United States should take the initiative in East-West exchanges as a positive instrument of U.S. foreign policy, employing as a general guide the 17-point proposal (attached) as submitted at the Geneva Foreign Ministers meeting. Each proposal should be judged on its merits as contributing to the agreed objectives.

17. The United States should make clear as appropriate to third countries the scope and purpose of our programs.

Seventeen-Point Proposal Submitted
at the Geneva Foreign Ministers Meeting

1. Freer exchange of information and ideas should be facilitated. All censorship should be progressively eliminated. The obstacles which hamper the flow of full factual information and varied comment between the peoples of the West and those of the Soviet Union, should be removed.

2. Arrangements should be made for the four Powers to open information centers, on a basis of reciprocity, in each other's capitals where these do not already exist. Everyone should be allowed full use of these centers without hindrance or discouragement from their own government.

3. The four Powers, where they do not already do so, should permit the publication and facilitate the distribution to public institutions and private individuals in each other's countries of official periodicals printed in English, French or Russian.

4. Exchange of books, periodicals and newspapers between the principal libraries, universities and professional and scientific bodies in the Soviet Union and the three Western countries should be encouraged. Such books, periodicals and newspapers should also be available for general and unimpeded public sale in the Soviet Union on the one hand and the three Western countries on the other.

5. There should be a substantial increase in the exchange of government publications and full lists, catalogs and indexes of such publications should be made available by Governments where they do not already do so.

6. The film producers of the three Western countries are ready to make films available to the Soviet Union at normal commercial prices and on normal commercial terms. Soviet films are already accepted in the West on these terms.

7. There should be exchanges of exhibitions between the Soviet Union and the three Western countries.

8. The systematic jamming of broadcasts of news and information is a practice to be deplored. It is incompatible with the Directive from the Four Heads of Government and should be discontinued.

9. The Soviet Union and the Western Powers should consider the desirability of monthly uncensored broadcasts on world developments. This could take the form of half hours for the Soviet Union on the Western broadcasting systems with reciprocal arrangements for the Western Powers on the Soviet system.

10. The censorship of outgoing press despatches and the denial to journalists of access to normal sources of information are serious barriers to the free circulation of ideas. The four Governments, where appropriate, should take immediate steps to remove such barriers.

11. Private tourism should be increased. This will require more liberal procedures as regards travel restrictions and other administrative practices. Above all it will require reasonable rates of currency exchange.

12. There should be further exchanges of persons in the professional, cultural, scientific and technical fields. Exchanges should be arranged on the basis of principles approved by the governments concerned.

13. Meetings of outstanding scientists and scholars of the four countries at reputable international congresses should be facilitated.

14. There should be cultural and sporting exchanges on a reciprocal basis, drawing on the best each has to offer under the auspices of the principal cultural institutions and sporting organizations on both sides.

15. A beginning should be made with exchanges of students, particularly those engaged in language and other area studies. It should be possible for the students to share fully and freely the student life of the country they visit.

16. Restrictions on the ability of the members of the diplomatic missions of the four governments to travel in each other's countries should be removed on a basis of reciprocity.

17. Agreement should be reached in principle for reciprocal exchanges of direct air transport services between cities of the Soviet Union and cities of the three Western countries.

This document, obtained under the Freedom of Information Act, was declassified and released by the Department of State on December 24, 1984. It was transcribed from a copy of the original.

Appendix B:
U.S.-USSR General Agreement
of November 21, 1985
and Program of Cooperation
and Exchanges for 1986-1988

THE GENERAL AGREEMENT
BETWEEN THE GOVERNMENT OF
THE UNITED STATES OF AMERICA
AND THE GOVERNMENT OF
THE UNION OF SOVIET SOCIALIST REPUBLICS
ON CONTACTS, EXCHANGES, AND COOPERATION
IN SCIENTIFIC, TECHNICAL, EDUCATIONAL,
CULTURAL AND OTHER FIELDS

The Government of the United States of America and the Government of the Union of Soviet Socialist Republics;

Desiring to promote better understanding between the peoples of the United States of America and the Union of Soviet Socialist Republics and to help improve the general state of relations between the two countries;

Referring to the relevant principles, provisions and objectives set forth in the Final Act of the Conference on Security and Cooperation in Europe;

Consistent with the relevant provisions of the Basic Principles of Relations Between the United States of America and the Union of Soviet Socialist Republics, signed at Moscow on May 29, 1972;

Believing that the further expansion of reciprocal and mutually beneficial contacts, exchanges and cooperation will facilitate the achievement of these aims;

Taking into account the positive experience achieved through previous agreements on exchanges in the cultural, educational, scientific and technical fields, and in other fields;

Have agreed as follows:

ARTICLE I

1. The Parties will encourage and develop contacts, exchanges and cooperation in the fields of the natural sciences, technology, the humanities and social sciences, education, culture, and in other fields of mutual interest on the basis of equality, mutual benefit, and reciprocity.

2. This General Agreement and implementation of the contacts, exchanges and cooperation under it shall be subject to the Constitution and applicable laws and regulations of the respective countries. Within this framework, the Parties will take all appropriate measures to ensure favorable conditions for such contacts, exchanges and cooperation, and the safety of, and normal working conditions for, those participating in American-Soviet exchanges.

ARTICLE II

1. The Parties take note of the following specialized agreements on cooperation in various fields and reaffirm their commitments to achieve their fulfillment and to encourage the renewal or extension of them, when it is considered mutually beneficial:

a. The Agreement on Cooperation in the Field of Environmental Protection between the United States of America and the Union of Soviet Socialist Republics, signed at Moscow on May 23, 1972, and extended until May 23, 1987, by means of an exchange of Diplomatic Notes;

b. The Agreement between the Government of the United States of America and the Government of the Union of Soviet Socialist Republics on Cooperation in the Field of Medical Science and Public Health, signed at Moscow on May 23, 1972, and extended until May 23, 1987, by means of an exchange of Diplomatic Notes;

c. The Agreement between the Government of the United States of America and the Government of the Union of Soviet Socialist Republics on Cooperation in the Field of Agriculture, signed at Washington on June 19, 1973, and extended until June 19, 1988, by means of an exchange of Diplomatic Notes;

d. The Agreement between the Government of the United States of America and the Government of the Union of Soviet Socialist

Republics on Cooperation in Studies of the World Ocean, signed at Washington on June 19, 1973, and extended until December 14, 1987, by means of an exchange of Diplomatic Notes;

e. The Agreement between the United States of America and the Union of Soviet Socialist Republics on Scientific and Technical Cooperation in the Field of Peaceful Uses of Atomic Energy, signed at Washington on June 21, 1973, and extended until June 20, 1986, by means of an exchange of Diplomatic Notes;

f. The Agreement between the United States of America and the Union of Soviet Socialist Republics on Cooperation in the Field of Housing and Other Construction, signed at Moscow on June 28, 1974, and extended until June 28, 1989, by means of an exchange of Diplomatic Notes;

g. The Agreement between the United States of America and the Union of Soviet Socialist Republics on Cooperation in Artificial Heart Research and Development, signed at Moscow on June 28, 1974, and extended until June 28, 1987, by means of an exchange of Diplomatic Notes;

h. The Long Term Agreement between the United States of America and the Union of Soviet Socialist Republics to Facilitate Economic, Industrial, and Technical Cooperation, signed at Moscow on June 29, 1974, and extended until June 28, 1994, by means of an exchange of Diplomatic Notes;

2. When it is considered mutually beneficial, the Parties will encourage within the framework of this Agreement conclusion of specialized agreements, including renewal and mutually agreed amendments, between:

a. The National Academy of Sciences of the United States of America and the Academy of Sciences of the Union of Soviet Socialist Republics;

b. The American Council of Learned Societies and the Academy of Sciences of the Union of Soviet Socialist Republics;

c. Institutions of higher education of both countries.

3. The Parties will encourage the conclusion, when it is considered mutually beneficial, of agreements on cooperation in the field of science and technology, and also additional agreements in other specialized fields, including the humanities and social sciences, within the framework of this Agreement.

ARTICLE III

The Parties will encourage and facilitate, as appropriate, contacts, exchanges and cooperation between organizations of the two countries in the fields of the humanities and social sciences, natural sciences, technology, education, and in other related fields of mutual interest which are not being carried out under specialized agreements concluded between the Parties. These activities may include:

1. The exchange of experts, delegations, scholarly and technical information, the organization of lectures, seminars and symposia for such experts;

2. The participation of scholars and other specialists in professional congresses, conferences and similar meetings being held in the two countries, and the conducting of specialized exhibits and of joint research work;

3. Other forms of contacts, exchanges and cooperation which may be mutually agreed upon.

ARTICLE IV

1. The Parties will encourage and facilitate, as appropriate, contacts, exchanges and cooperation between organizations of the two countries in various fields of education. These activities may include:

a. The exchange of students, graduate students, researchers and faculty members for study and research; the exchange of professors and teachers to lecture, offer instruction, and conduct research; the exchange of specialists and delegations in various fields of education; and, as possible, the organization of lectures, seminars and symposia for such specialists;

b. The exchange of more young researchers preparing dissertations, as well as of young teachers, taking into account the desirability of proper representation of the social sciences, the humanities, and the natural and applied sciences in these exchanges;

c. Making available to students, researchers and teachers appropriate educational, research and open archive materials which are relevant to the agreed topic of research based, as a minimum, upon the agreed preliminary plan of study and, as possible, other resources which may come to light during the course of the researcher's stay;

d. The facilitation of the exchange, by appropriate organizations, of educational and teaching materials (including textbooks, syllabi and curricula), materials on methodology, samples of teaching instruments and audiovisual aids.

2. The Parties will also encourage the study of each other's languages through the development of the exchanges and cooperation listed above and through other mutually agreed measures.

ARTICLE V

1. In order to promote better acquaintance with the cultural achievements of each country, the Parties will facilitate the reciprocal development of contacts, exchanges and artistic cooperation in the field of the performing arts. To these ends the Parties will assist exchanges of theatrical, musical, and choreographic ensembles, orchestras, and other performing and artistic groups, as well as individual directors and performers.

ARTICLE VI

1. The Parties will encourage the film industries of both countries, as appropriate, to consider means of further expanding the purchase and distribution on a commercial basis of films produced in each country; the joint production of feature, documentary, popular-science, and educational films; and the rendering, upon request, of production and creative assistance by each side for films produced by the other.

2. The Parties will encourage as appropriate, the exchange and exhibition of documentary films dealing with science, technology, culture, education and other fields.

3. The Parties will render assistance to the exchange of delegations of creative workers and technical experts in various aspects of film-making.

4. The Parties also agree to consider, at the request of organizations or individuals of their own countries, other proposals for the expansion of mutually acceptable exchanges in this field, including holding film premieres and film weeks, and participating in international film festivals held in each country.

ARTICLE VII

1. The Parties will, on a mutually acceptable basis, assist contacts and encourage exchanges between organizations of both countries in the field of radio and television, including exchanges of radio programs and television films, both for educational purposes and for transmission to local audiences, and in addition exchanges of delegations of creative workers and technical specialists in various fields of radio and television broadcasting. Appearances of representatives of each country on television of the other country can take place in accordance with the existing practices and regulations of each country.

2. The Parties further agree, upon the request of organizations and individuals of their own countries, to consider other proposals in the field of radio and television, including joint production of television films and rendering services in the production of radio and television programs. Each Party, as possible and in accordance with the relevant laws and regulations of the receiving country, will render assistance to the other in the preparation of such programs.

ARTICLE VIII

The Parties note that in the pursuit of better mutual understanding, a desirable goal is the greater familiarity of each country's people with the literature and other publications of the other. To this end, the Parties will encourage:

1. The exchange of book exhibits, literary works, magazines, newspapers and other publications devoted to scholarly, technical, cultural, and general educational subjects between libraries, universities and other organizations of each country, as well as the reciprocal distribution of the magazines *Amerika* and *Soviet Life;*

2. Exchanges and visits of journalists, editors and publishers, translators of literary works, as well as their participation in appropriate professional meetings and conferences;

3. Further development of cooperation between publishing houses of the two countries, when such expansion is seen as useful to it by individual publishing houses or their professional organizations.

ARTICLE IX

1. The Parties will encourage and facilitate the exchange of exhibitions on various topics of mutual interest. The Parties agree to accord each other the opportunity for two to four circulating exhibitions during the six-year period of this Agreement.

2. The Parties will encourage and facilitate appropriate participation by one Party in exhibitions which may take place in the other's country.

3. The Parties will also render assistance for the exchange of exhibitions between the museums of the two countries.

ARTICLE X

The Parties will provide for mutually acceptable exchanges, cooperation and visits of architects, art historians, artists, composers, musicologists, museum specialists, playwrights, theater directors, writers, specialists in various fields of law, including public law and government, and those in other cultural and professional fields, to familiarize themselves with matters of interest to them in their respective fields and to participate in meetings, conferences and symposia.

ARTICLE XI

1. The Parties will render assistance to members of the Congress of the United States of America and Deputies of the Supreme Soviet of the Union of Soviet Socialist Republics, as well as to officials of the National Government of both countries making visits to the Union of Soviet Socialist Republics and the United States of America, respectively. Arrangements for such assistance will be agreed upon in advance through diplomatic channels.

2. The Parties will encourage exchanges of representatives of municipal, local and state governments of the United States of America and the Union of Soviet Socialist Republics to study various functions of government at these levels.

ARTICLE XII

The Parties will encourage joint undertakings and exchanges between appropriate organizations active in civic and social life, including youth and women's organizations, recognizing that the decision to implement such joint undertakings and exchanges remains a concern of the organizations themselves.

ARTICLE XIII

The Parties will encourage the development of contacts in sports through organizing competitions, exchanging delegations, teams, athletes and coaches in the field of physical culture and sports upon agreement between the appropriate sports organizations of both countries.

ARTICLE XIV

The Parties will encourage the expansion of tourism between the two countries with the aim of more fully satisfying the requests of tourists to become acquainted with the life, work and culture of the people of each country. In this connection the Parties will encourage, on a mutually acceptable basis, tourist trips, on a group and individual basis, thus to facilitate exchanges between young people, workers, farmers and representatives of other vocations.

ARTICLE XV

The Parties will encourage the further development of contacts and cooperation between archival organizations of the two countries. Initial program proposals on these contacts and cooperation will be made through diplomatic channels.

ARTICLE XVI

The Parties note that commemorative activities may take place in their countries in connection with the celebration of anniversaries recognized by major international bodies.

ARTICLE XVII

The Parties agree that, as necessary, they will hold meetings of their representatives for the general review of the implementation of contacts, exchanges and cooperation in various fields and to consider the possibility of exchanges which are not carried out under specialized agreements between the two Parties. These reviews, which may be requested by either side, will take place usually annually but at least once during the period of each three-year Program.

ARTICLE XVIII

The Parties agree that:

1. The programs and itineraries, lengths of stay, dates of arrival, size of delegations, financial and transportation arrangements and other details of exchanges and visits, except as otherwise determined, shall be agreed upon, as a rule, not less than thirty days in advance, through diplomatic channels or between appropriate organizations requested by the Parties to carry out these exchanges;

2. Applications for visas for visitors participating in exchanges and cooperative activities shall be submitted, as a rule, at least ten working days before the estimated time of departure;

3. Unless otherwise provided for in specialized agreements between the Parties, and except where other specific arrangements have been agreed upon, participants in exchanges and cooperative

activities will pay their own expenses, including international travel, internal travel, and costs of maintenance in the receiving country.

ARTICLE XIX

1. In implementation of various provisions of this Agreement, the Parties have established a Program of Cooperation and Exchanges for 1986–88, which is attached and is an integral part of this Agreement. The terms of that Program shall be in force from January 1, 1986, to December 31, 1988, and thereafter, unless and until amended by agreement of the Parties, will provide the basic guidelines for the Program of Cooperation and Exchanges for 1989–1991.

2. The Parties agree that their representatives will meet prior to the end of 1988 to develop the Program of Cooperation and Exchanges for the succeeding three years.

ARTICLE XX

1. This Agreement shall enter into force on signature and shall remain in force until December 31, 1991. It may be modified or extended by mutual agreement of the Parties.

2. Nothing in this Agreement shall be construed to prejudice other agreements concluded between the two Parties.

DONE in Geneva this twenty-first day of November, 1985, in duplicate, in the English and Russian languages, both texts being equally authentic.

FOR THE GOVERNMENT OF THE   FOR THE GOVERNMENT OF
UNITED STATES OF AMERICA: THE UNION OF SOVIET
                                   SOCIALIST REPUBLICS:

[Signed by George P. Shultz]   [Signed by Eduard Shevardnadze]

PROGRAM OF COOPERATION AND EXCHANGES BETWEEN
THE UNITED STATES OF AMERICA AND
THE UNION OF SOVIET SOCIALIST REPUBLICS FOR 1986-1988

In implementation of various provisions of the General Agreement
between the United States of America and the Union of Soviet
Socialist Republics on Contacts, Exchanges and Cooperation in
Scientific, Technical, Educational, Cultural and Other Fields signed at
Geneva on November 21, 1985, the Parties have agreed on the
following Program of Exchanges.

ARTICLE I
HIGHER EDUCATION

1. The Parties will exchange annually from each side:
a. For long-term advanced research: At least 40 advanced
researchers, instructors and professors for study and scholarly research
in the humanities and the social, natural and applied sciences for
periods of from one semester to one academic year. For the purposes of
accounting, two stays of one semester each shall be equivalent to one
stay of one academic year.
b. For short-term advanced research: At least ten professors,
instructors and advanced researchers to conduct scholarly research in
the humanities and the social, natural and applied sciences for periods
of between two and five months.
c. At least 30 language teachers and two leaders from universities and other institutions of higher learning to participate in summer courses of two months to improve their competence in the language
of the receiving side.
d. Parallel to the exchanges specified under paragraphs a and
b above, the Parties note and encourage the exchange of scholars
between the American Council of Learned Societies and the Academy
of Sciences of the Union of Soviet Socialist Republics which involves
advanced research for up to 60 person-months from each side each
academic year.
e. The Parties affirm the reciprocal nature of these programs
in which the sending side chooses, at its own discretion, candidates for
participation in the exchanges, and the receiving side, at its
discretion, agrees to the placement of these candidates.
In this connection, the Parties note that, in the carrying out of the
exchanges specified under paragraphs 1a, b and c above and following
the existing practice of mutually acceptable participation in the
exchange of representatives in the humanities, social sciences, and

natural and technical sciences, they will strive, as in the past, for such mutually acceptable participation of scholars in the above-mentioned fields.

    f. In the practical implementation of these programs, the Parties will strive to maintain the levels of exchange already achieved, where the existing levels exceed the minimum levels given above.

    2. In accordance with the wishes of the sending and receiving sides, the Parties will exchange annually at least 15 professors and specialists from universities and other institutions of higher learning from each side. Both sides will attempt to include four lecturers on the languages and literatures of the sending side. The exchanges will be for periods of one to ten months, normally corresponding to the receiving side's academic calendar, to lecture and, as time permits, to teach and conduct research at universities and other institutions of higher learning.

The Parties note that this exchange has involved lecturers from a broad range of fields, corresponding to the needs of both sending and receiving sides. In this connection, the Parties will strive to maintain this mutually beneficial exchange in the various fields of the natural and technical sciences, the humanities, and the social sciences.

    3. The Parties will exchange during the period of this Program at least two delegations of specialists in higher education consisting of up to five persons from each side for periods of two to three weeks each, including two to three days of seminars with specialists of the other country. The subjects of the seminars and itineraries of the visits will be agreed upon subsequently.

    4. The Parties will encourage the conclusion of arrangements for direct exchanges between universities and other institutions of higher learning of the two countries for the purpose of study, research, lecturing, and participating in seminars. These exchanges would take place outside the exchange quotas mentioned in paragraphs 1, 2, and 3 above. They will be the subject of direct separate agreements concluded between the universities or institutes concerned, and the conditions for the exchanges listed above will not necessarily apply to them.

    5. The sides agree that the United States will continue to take measures to encourage the study of the Russian language in the United States of America, and the Soviet Union will continue its practice of teaching the English language in the Union of Soviet Socialist Republics. In order to realize the above goals, the Parties will encourage the expansion of exchange programs for language study whereby American and Soviet undergraduates can study Russian and English respectively, obtaining academic credits for that study.

6. The Parties agree to continue to exchange information and to conduct appropriate consultations regarding the equivalency of diplomas and scholarly degrees. The Parties expect that the Convention on the Recognition of Studies, Diplomas and Degrees Concerning Higher Education in the States Belonging to the Europe Region, in the elaboration of which the United States of America and the Union of Soviet Socialist Republics have taken part, will lead to closer cooperation in this field.

ARTICLE II
PRIMARY AND SECONDARY EDUCATION AND THE PEDAGOGICAL SCIENCES

1. The Parties will exchange annually from each side, groups of language teachers, up to a total of 15 persons, from secondary schools in the United States of America, and from secondary schools or pedagogical institutes in the Union of Soviet Socialist Republics, to participate in summer courses of six weeks duration, including up to two weeks of travel, to improve their competence in the teaching of the Russian and English languages and their knowledge of the Union of Soviet Socialist Republics and the United States of America. Each group of language teachers may be accompanied by a leader.

2. The Parties will exchange one delegation annually of specialists in primary and secondary education of up to five persons from each side for a period of two to three weeks each, including a seminar of normally two to three days with specialists of the other country. The subjects of the seminars, their duration and itineraries of the visits will be agreed upon subsequently.

3. The Parties will encourage the exchange of primary and secondary school textbooks and other teaching materials, and, as is deemed appropriate, the conducting of joint studies on textbooks, between appropriate organizations in the United States of America and the Ministry of Education of the Union of Soviet Socialist Republics.

ARTICLE III
ARTS AND CULTURE

1. The Parties agree to facilitate the tours of at least 10 major performing arts groups from each side during the period of this Program. If one Party sends more than 10 major performing arts groups, the other Party will be accorded the opportunity to send a like number of additional groups. The detailed arrangements for tours of these

groups will be provided for in contracts to be concluded between the following entities: for tours of American groups, between the Embassy of the United States of America in Moscow or authorized representatives of the groups, and concert organizations of the Union of Soviet Socialist Republics; for tours of Soviet groups, between appropriate organizations or impresarios of the United States of America and concert organizations of the Union of Soviet Socialist Republics. The receiving side, taking into consideration realistic possibilities, will seek to satisfy the wishes of the sending side concerning the timing and duration of the tours and the number of cities visited. The sending side shall provide timely notice in making proposals for performing arts groups to travel to the other country. The receiving side will make every effort to take a decision on each proposal by the sending side as soon as possible.

2. The Parties agree to facilitate the tours of at least 10 individual performers from each side during the period of this Program. If one Party sends more than 10 individual performers, the other Party will be accorded the opportunity to send a like number of individual performers. The detailed arrangements for these tours will be provided for in contracts to be concluded between the following entities: for tours of American performers, between the Embassy of the United States of America in Moscow or authorized representatives of the performers, and concert organizations of the Union of Soviet Socialist Republics; for tours of Soviet performers, between appropriate organizations or impresarios of the United States of America and concert organizations of the Union of Soviet Socialist Republics.

3. For the tours of the groups and individuals specified under paragraphs 1 and 2 above, the Parties will take all appropriate measures, to the extent permitted by the applicable laws and regulations, to ensure favorable conditions for these performances and tours, and for the safety of, and normal working conditions for, those participating in them.

4. The Parties will render assistance for the exchange of art exhibitions of equal quality or other exhibitions between museums of the two countries, on the basis of reciprocity where possible, and will encourage the establishment and development of direct contacts between these museums with the aim of exchanging informative materials, albums, art monographs and other publications of mutual interest. In the case of art exhibitions, their content and the conditions for conducting them, including questions of financial responsibility of governments in the event of loss or damage, guarantees of appropriate safety precautions and timely return, and immunity from seizure on the part of possible previous owners will be the subject of negotiation

between appropriate museums or interested organizations of the United States of America and the Ministry of Culture of the Union of Soviet Socialist Republics, and special agreements between them will be signed in each specific case. Within this process, the possible need for added safety precautions to include additional guards at the exhibit sites, will be addressed as required: in the United States of America by the Indemnity Advisory Panel reporting to the Federal Council on the Arts and Humanities, and in the Union of Soviet Socialist Republics by comparable organizations responsible for the safety of foreign exhibits.

5. The Parties will encourage exchanges of delegations and individual specialists in various fields of art and culture, including, among others, such fields as libraries, museums, music, theater, fine arts, architecture and historic preservation and restoration.

6. The Parties will encourage and facilitate exchanges of theater directors, composers, choreographers, stage designers, performers, musicians and other creative artists for production in performances, with due concern for, and encouragement of, the production of the works of the sending country. The conditions for these exchanges will be agreed upon on a case-by-case basis. Both sides will strive to maintain mutually acceptable exchanges over the course of this Program.

ARTICLE IV
PUBLICATIONS

The Parties agree to render practical assistance for the distribution of the magazines *Amerika* in the Union of Soviet Socialist Republics and *Soviet Life* in the United States of America on the basis of reciprocity and to consult as necessary in order to find ways to increase the distribution of these magazines. Upon reaching full distribution of the 62,000 copies of each magazine as currently provided for, the Parties will examine the possibility of expanding the reciprocal distribution of the magazines to 82,000. The Parties will distribute free of charge unsold copies of the magazines among visitors to mutually arranged exhibitions.

ARTICLE V
EXHIBITIONS

1. The Parties agree to accord each other the opportunity for 1 to 2 circulating exhibitions during the three-year period of this Program. Each Party will accord the other the opportunity to show its exhibition or exhibitions in 6 to 9 cities in all, with up to 28 showing

days in each city. The number of cities and number of showing days, up to the maxima noted above, will be determined by the sending side. The subjects of the exhibitions will be agreed upon through diplomatic channels. The Parties will discuss in a preliminary fashion the nature and general content of each exhibition and will acquaint each other with the exhibitions before their official opening, in particular through the exchange of catalogues, prospectuses and other information pertinent to the exhibitions. Other conditions for conducting the exhibitions (precise opening and closing dates, size and character of the premises, number of personnel, financial terms, etc.) shall be subject to agreement by the Parties. Arrangements for conducting the exhibitions shall be concluded no later than five months before their opening.

2. The Parties will agree through diplomatic channels on arrangements for other exhibitions and on participation in national exhibitions which may take place in either country.

ARTICLE VI
OTHER EXCHANGES

1. The Parties will encourage cooperation between organizations of both countries in the field of radio and television, including exchanges of radio and television programs, the joint production of films and broadcasts, the exchange of delegations and specialists, and, in addition, at the request of organizations and individuals, will consider other types of activities provided for in Article VII of the General Agreement.

2. The Parties will encourage invitations to journalists for familiarization with the print and broadcast media in the receiving country. To this end, the Parties will facilitate the exchange of at least three journalists annually from each side.

3. The Parties will encourage exchanges and contacts in the field of book publishing and translation. Among the desired goals of such exchanges would be mutually acceptable programs which would expand the scope of one country's literature and publications available in translation in the other. Such program decisions would be taken by the appropriate organizations or publishing houses of the two countries.

4. The Parties will encourage the mutually acceptable exchange of films and film specialists, the joint production of films, the rendering of production and creative assistance for films produced by each country and the holding of film premieres, film weeks, seminars and other film events on an annual basis. The Parties will also consider additional

proposals aimed at expanding cooperation, as referred to in Article VI of the General Agreement. Conditions for implementing exchanges in this field will be determined by mutual agreement.

5.   The Parties recognize the value of visits by other specialists in addition to those noted elsewhere in this Program, for lectures and participation in seminars, meetings and discussions which contribute to better understanding between the peoples of the two countries.

6.   In accordance with Article XV of the General Agreement, the Parties will facilitate the development of contacts and cooperation between the archival institutions of the two countries, and will encourage the conclusion of mutually beneficial exchange agreements. In particular, the Parties will encourage the reestablishment of close contacts between the Main Archival Administration under the Council of Ministers of the Union of Soviet Socialist Republics and the National Archives of the United States of America.

7.   The Parties will encourage, on a mutually acceptable basis, the expansion of exchanges between young people, workers, farmers and representatives of other vocations.

8.   The Parties will encourage continuing contacts between the organizations referred to in Article XII of the General Agreement. Terms of these exchanges will be determined by mutual agreement.

ARTICLE VII
GENERAL PROVISIONS

1.   This Program and the exchanges and visits provided for herein shall be subject to the Constitution and applicable laws and regulations of the two countries.   Within this framework, both Parties will take all appropriate measures to ensure favorable conditions for such cooperation, exchanges and visits, and the safety of, and normal working conditions for, those participating in U.S.-Soviet exchanges in accordance with the provisions and objectives of this Program and the General Agreement.

2.   The Parties agree to hold periodic meetings of their representatives to discuss the implementation of the Program.   The implementation reviews will be held at times and places to be agreed upon through diplomatic channels.

3.   Each of the Parties shall have the right to include in delegations interpreters or members of its Embassy, who would be considered as within the agreed total membership of such delegations. The number of such persons shall in each specific case be decided by mutual agreement.

4.   This Program is valid from January 1, 1986, through December 31, 1988.

DONE at Geneva, this twenty-first day of November, 1985, in duplicate, in the English and Russian languages, both texts being equally authentic.

FOR THE GOVERNMENT OF THE UNITED STATES OF AMERICA:	FOR THE GOVERNMENT OF THE UNION OF SOVIET SOCIALIST REPUBLICS:
[Signed by George P. Shultz]	[Signed by Eduard Shevardnadze]

The documents in this Appendix were transcribed from copies of the originals, but have been single- rather than double-spaced.

An Annex to the Program of Cooperation and Exchanges for 1986–1988, which is not reproduced here, contains details of the administrative and financial terms of the exchanges specified in the Program. Copies of the Annex may be obtained from the United States Information Agency, Washington, D.C.

Glossary

AAASS	American Association for the Advancement of Slavic Studies
ACLS	American Council of Learned Societies
ACYPL	American Council of Young Political Leaders
CIA	Central Intelligence Agency
CIEE	Council on International Educational Exchange
CIES	Council for International Exchange of Scholars
COMEX	Committee on Exchanges
CSCE	Conference on Security and Cooperation in Europe
Goskontsert	State Concert Agency
ICCUSA	Interagency Coordinating Committee for U.S.-Soviet Affairs
IREX	International Research and Exchanges Board
IUCTG	Inter-University Committee on Travel Grants
KGB	Committee on State Security
KKI	Hungarian Cultural Institute
MPAA	Motion Picture Association of America
NATO	North Atlantic Treaty Organization
NSC	National Security Council
S & T	Science and Technology
SSRC	Social Science Research Council
SUNY	State University of New York
TIAS	Treaties and Other International Acts Series
U.S.C.	United States Code
UNA	United Nations Association of the United States of America
USIA	United States Information Agency

Bibliography

A Balance Sheet for East-West Exchanges. IREX Occasional Papers 1, no. 1. New York: International Research and Exchanges Board, 1980.

Basket III: Implementation of the Helsinki Accords, Information Flow, and Cultural and Educational Exchanges. Hearings Before the Commission on Security and Cooperation in Europe, May 19, 24 and 25, 1977. Washington, D.C.. U.S. Government Printing Office, 1977.

Berman, Maureen R., and Johnson, Joseph E. *Unofficial Diplomats.* New York: Columbia University Press, 1977.

Brod, Richard I., and Devens, Monica S. "Foreign Language Enrollments in U.S. Institutions of Higher Education—Fall 1983, *ADFL Bulletin* 16, no. 2 (January 1985).

Byrnes, Robert F. *Soviet-American Academic Exchanges, 1958–1975.* Bloomington: Indiana University Press, 1976.

"Conference on Security and Cooperation in Europe: Final Act," *Department of State Bulletin, September 1, 1975.*

Eisenhower, Dwight D. *Waging Peace, 1956–1961.* Garden City: Doubleday, 1965.

Exchanges of U.S.-U.S.S.R. Officials. Hearing Before the Committee on Foreign Relations, United States Senate, 91st Cong. 2d sess., on S. 3127, To Provide for the Exchange of Government Officials Between the United States and the Union of Soviet Socialist Republics. Washington, D.C.: U.S. Government Printing Office, 1970.

Gaer, Felice D. "Soviet-American Scholarly Exchanges: Should Learning and Politics Mix?" *Vital Issues* 29, no. 10 (June 1980)

Graham, Loren R. "How Valuable are Scientific Exchanges with the Soviet Unon?" *Science* 20 (October 27, 1978).

The Helsinki Forum and East-West Scientific Exchange. Joint Hearings before Two Subcommittees of the Committee on Foreign Affairs, U.S. House of Representatives and the Commission on Security and Cooperation in Europe. Washington, D.C.: U.S. Government Printing Office, 1980.

Implementation of the Final Act of the Conference on Security and Cooperation in Europe: Findings and Recommendations Five Years After Helsinki. A Report Submitted to the Congress by the Commission on Security and Cooperation in Europe. Washington, D.C.: U.S. Government Printing Office, 1980.

Joyce, John M. "U.S.-Soviet Science Exchanges: A Foot in the Soviet Door." Paper no. 11 in the "Soviet Science and Technology: Eyewitness Accounts" Seminar. Cambridge: Russian Research Center, Harvard University, 1981.

Kadushin, Charles; Denitch, Bogdan; and Genevie, Louise. *An Evaluation of the Experience of Exchange Participants, 1969–70 through 1974–75* . New York: International Research and Exchanges Board, 1977.

Kampelman, Max M. "An Assessment of the Madrid CSCE Followup Meeting." *Department of State Bulletin, September 1983.*

Key Issues in U.S.-U.S.S.R. Scientific Exchanges and Technology Transfer. A Report Prepared by the Subcommittee on Science, Research and Technology of the Committee on Science and Technology, U.S. House of Representatives. Washington, D.C.: U.S. Government Printing Office, 1979.

Levin, Martin P. "Soviet International Copyright: Dream or Nightmare?" *Journal of the Copyright Society of America,* December 1983, no. 2.

Lottman, Herbert R., "The Soviet Way of Publishing," *Publishers Weekly,* November 8, 1976.

Lubrano, Linda L. "The Political Web of Scientific Cooperation Between the U.S.A. and USSR." In *Sectors of Mutual Benefit in U.S.-Soviet Relations,* edited by Nish Jamgotch, Jr. Durham: Duke University Press, 1985.

Maresca, John J. *To Helsinki—The Conference on Security and Cooperation in Europe, 1973–75.* Durham: Duke University Press, 1985.

Marks, Leonard H., and Smith, William French. *The Effects of the Conference on Security and Cooperation in Europe on the Cultural Relations of the United States and Eastern Europe.* A Special Report to Congress from the United States Advisory Commission on International Educational and Cultural Affairs, April 1976. Washington, D.C.: U.S. Government Printing Office, 1976.

NSC 5607, "East-West Exchanges." National Security Council statement of policy, June 29, 1956; declassified and released under the Freedom of Information Act, December 24, 1984.

Open Doors: Report on International Educational Exchange, 1983/84 . New York: Institute of International Education, 1984.

Overview of International Science and Technology Policy. Hearings before the Subcommittees on International Security and Scientific Affairs, Committee on Foreign Affairs, House of Representatives, August 2, 1983. Washington, D.C.: U.S. Government Printing Office, 1983.

Perspectives: Relations Between the United States and the Soviet Union. Washington, D.C.: U.S. Government Printing Office, 1979.

The Raised Curtain. Report of the Twentieth Century Fund Task Force on Soviet-American Scholarly and Cultural Exchanges. New York: The Twentieth Century Fund, 1977.

Report on Exchanges with the Soviet Union and Eastern Europe. A series of status reports listing all U.S. exchanges with the Soviet Union under the cultural agreement and the countries of Eastern Europe, prepared by the Soviet and Eastern European Exchanges Staff, Department of State. Washington, D.C.: U.S. Government Printing Office, various years through the mid-1970s.

Review of U.S.-U.S.S.R. Interacademy Exchanges and Relations. Washington, D.C.: National Academy of Sciences, 1977.

Richmond, Yale. *Soviet-American Cultural Exchanges: Ripoff or Payoff?* Washington, D.C.: Woodrow Wilson International Center for Scholars, 1984.

Russian Language Study in the United States. Stanford: American Association for the Advancement of Slavic Studies, 1983.

Saunders, Harold H. "When Citizens Talk: A Look at Nonofficial Dialogue in Relations Between Nations." *The Kettering Review,* Summer 1984.

Scientific Communication and National Security. 2 vols. Washington, D.C.: National Academy Press, 1982.

Soviet-American Exchange and Human Rights: A Conference Report and Nine Case Studies. New York: U.S. Helsinki Watch Committee, 1980.

Survey of U.S. Educational and Cultural Exchanges with the Soviet Union and Eastern Europe. A classified report prepared by Boris H. Klosson for the Department of State, June 23, 1978, declassified and released under the Freedom of Information Act, December 24, 1984.

Talbott, Strobe, ed. & tr. *Khrushchev Remembers: The Last Testament* . Boston: Little Brown and Co., 1974.

Transfer of U.S. High Technology to the Soviet Union and Soviet Bloc Nations . Hearings before the Senate Permanent Subcommittee on Investigations of the Committee on Government Affairs, U.S. Senate, May 1982. Washington, D.C.: U.S. Government Printing Office, 1982.

United States Treaties and Other International Agreements. Washington, D.C.: U.S. Government Printing Office.

U.S.-Soviet Agreements and Relationships. A report by the Congressional Research Service, October 16, 1978,. Washington, D.C.: The Library of Congress.

U.S.-Soviet Exchanges, A Conference Report. Washington, D.C.: Woodrow Wilson International Center for Scholars, 1985.

Vishnevskaya, Galina. *A Russian Story,* New York: Harcourt Brace Jovanovich, 1984.

Wiley, Bradford, and Hoopes, Townsend. "A Publishing Summit in Moscow." *Publishers Weekly,* November 8, 1976.

Index